Self-Discipline

A Guide to Building Self-Discipline and Achieving Your Goals In Life

Ethan Pitt

Copyright © Ethan Pitt Publishing

All rights reserved.
No part of this publication may be reproduced, distributed, or transmitted in any form or by any means, including photocopying, recording, or other electronic or mechanical methods, without the prior written permission of the publisher, except in the case of brief quotations embodied in critical reviews and certain other non-commercial uses permitted by copyright law.

Table of Contents

Become A More Self-Disciplined, Calm and Confident Person..4

Real Life Case Study - Gabriella 7

Chapter 1 : Let's Build Self-Discipline 9

The Effective Models We Can Use...................14

Real Life Case Study – Justin 18

Chapter 2 : This Can Change Everything..................21

Taming Negative Self-Talk with NLP Techniques...........24

Easy Exercises To Help You Everyday 29

Real Life Case Study – Sarah............................32

Chapter 3 : Easy To Follow Steps To Become Stronger ...35

Dealing With Stress 36

Dealing with Diet & Exercise...........................42

Real Life Case Study – Nikhil...........................47

Chapter 4 : Easily Set Goals & Motivators......................50

The Right Way To Set Goals – And Stick To Them! 54

Maintaining Focus On Goals............................56

Real Life Case Study – Daniel...........................62

Chapter 5 : Quickly Gain Motivation & Improve Dedication To Dealing With Habits........................64

The Simple and Effective Guide To Forming Habits 66
Real Life Case Study – James 74

Chapter 6 : Lessons From The Unexpected 77
Real Life Case Study - John..85

Chapter 7 : Defeating The Enemy; Procrastination.........88
Taking Back Control 93
Real Life Case Study – Julia 97

Chapter 8 : Three Key Steps to Self-Discipline...............100
Real Life Case Study – Julia 111

Chapter 9 : Maintaining Momentum 114
What To Do When Momentum Stops 118
Real Life Case Study – The Magic Of Momentum 123

Conclusion: Your New Level of Self-Discipline Starts Here
....125

Become A More Self-Disciplined, Calm and Confident Person

Self-discipline. It's the key to good health and great success. Most of us feel like we need more of it, and we all know at least one person who we believe has lots of it. But what is it?

The dictionary definition is: *"The ability to control one's feelings and overcome one's weaknesses."*

Self-discipline is the ability to get things done, without succumbing to your personal wants and feelings about the task at hand. It's both incredibly simple and incredibly complicated. When you are self-disciplined, you are able to control any nonconstructive urges, and can diligently work towards your goals. We often think academic intelligence is the key to academic achievement; empathy the key to great relationships; and charisma the success behind great leaders. Yet, some interesting studies have shown that the real key to all these things may be… you guessed it, *self-discipline*.

In a simple delayed gratification test, young pre-school age children were sat in a room, in front of a delicious treat like a marshmallow. The children were told they would be left alone in the room for a short while. They could eat the treat while the researcher was out of the room but if they chose not to, they would be rewarded by having two treats instead when the researcher returned. They were then left for approximately ten minutes alone with the treat. Interestingly, the children that waited for the longest and didn't eat the treat were more likely to go on to achieve higher grades in school. They also had better stress responses and higher social competence. The researchers determined that this was potentially down to their high level of self-control.

We often assume being self-disciplined means we need to spend a lot of time doing things we dislike, or even that self-disciplined people are boring. Luckily that's not true. When you have good self-discipline, implemented correctly, it actually creates joy and happiness rather than depleting it.

Another myth is that self-discipline is something you either have, or you lack. Again, that's not true at all. Self-discipline is very much a skill that you can learn and develop, no matter your starting point. In fact, it's an essential skill to develop if you want to be successful, productive, and happy.

When you are self-disciplined, you naturally make better choices because you are not succumbing to impulse decisions based on emotions. Self-disciplined people are clear on their goals and how to achieve them. They are also better able to weigh up how their actions will help or hinder progress towards their goals. Self-discipline also helps you stand strong in the face of adversity and weather any hardships and obstacles that may come your way.

Studies have confirmed that self-discipline increases happiness. One study conducted in 2013 by **Wilhelm Hofmann** showed that participants who had high self-control were happier compared to those who had lower restraint.

According to the results of this study, people with high self-control handle obstacles much better, are less likely to partake in unhealthy behaviors and are more easily able to make positive decisions.

This book is designed to give you the skills and resources you need to become more self-disciplined in your everyday life. In the following chapters we will cover:
- Why you need self-discipline
- The science and psychology behind self-discipline
- How to develop self-discipline
- How to maintain self-discipline

When you have finished reading you will:
- Understand the reasons behind poor self-discipline
- Understand the science and psychology behind laziness and procrastination
- Have the tools and strategies you need to become disciplined and start achieving more.

The very first thing you'll need is the will to develop self-discipline. Luckily, by picking up this book, you've demonstrated that you do have the desire to improve. Let's get started!

Real Life Case Study - Gabriella

Gabriella, a medical student, was envious of her friends who seemed to be more self-disciplined than she was. She wanted to develop a healthy, active lifestyle but felt she lacked the willpower and self-discipline to make the changes she needed to make. She worked shifts as well as studying and fitting in exercise seemed too difficult. Junk food was an easy convenience on work days, and it seemed difficult to break the habit by preparing healthy meals to take to work or college.

She was in a cycle of eating unhealthily and feeling low. She knew her diet was harming her health, and she felt lazy for being 'unable' to make the changes she wanted to. She attempted a handful of extreme 'boot camp' style health programs, but they never seemed to stick. She asked her friends how they were so self-disciplined to stick with their healthy lifestyles. They explained it was something they had to develop and not something that came naturally to them.

This was a new concept to Gabriella, but it was one that gave her hope. She researched how to develop self-discipline and came across numerous tools and ways to improve your self-discipline. She realized that her previous attempts had failed because she was approaching it in the wrong way. By starting small and building up, she was able to find the willpower to change both her diet and implement an exercise routine. Over the course of 12 months, she developed healthy and sustainable habits that, supplemented by her newfound self-discipline, she was confident she could maintain indefinitely.

Gabriella's story isn't uncommon. Many people, once they realize that they are not inherently lazy or lacking in willpower, take positive steps to develop self-discipline, and experience amazing transformations. Your personal journey to self-discipline might be a little different, but the overall results will be the same. If you follow the advice and tools laid out in this book, you will quickly start to see how you are able to complete tasks and achieve goals. Even ones that previously seemed out of your reach.

Chapter 1 : Let's Build Self-Discipline

Why Self-Discipline Matters

Why is it so hard to be self-disciplined? It's common for people to believe they are lazy if they are unable to get on and do the tasks and activities they may not necessarily enjoy. The actual answer is a little more complicated than just laziness. But *why?*

What makes it so impossible to stop smoking or start an exercise program?

What makes you choose to watch TV instead of starting work on that side hustle you've been dreaming of doing?

Why do you procrastinate on writing the book you've always wanted to write?

These are all things you might want to do, but you just can't commit to getting started. Or even worse, you start but then abandon your plan at the first sign of difficulty. You have big goals that you need to achieve, and all it takes is a little self-discipline. So, why is your self-discipline so lacking?

Our modern-day lives give us opportunities and experiences that weren't possible just 25 years ago. Yet along with the positive opportunities, there are also downsides to the expansion of our world. Before our lives were so public and online via social media, it was much harder to compare yourself to others. It was also much harder for people to project an image of themselves that was skewed from reality.

Consider any people you may look up to but only know via their online or public persona. Perhaps they are a successful and charismatic entrepreneur or a health and fitness influencer. They make what they do look effortless and are sharing seemingly never-ending success online. Consider that while they may be super successful, what you see is only ever what they want you to see. Things may not be exactly as they seem. Yet we constantly compare our own lives to theirs. Feeling the pressure to live a perfect life, be wealthy, healthy and super-successful is an ever-present burden.

Add to that, the constant marketing and advertising techniques we are subjected to every single day. Marketing often relies on tactics specifically designed to subvert your self-control and tap into your impulses. There's even an entire branch of marketing called neuromarketing, dedicated to studying and using your brain's natural wiring to sell you more stuff.

Of course, once you're aware of these tactics and how they work, you can be on the lookout for them. But as we'll discuss in a moment – the sheer amount of them can drain your willpower. So, while you may resist the first temptation placed in front of you, by the fiftieth, you may be much more likely to give in. We're exposed every day to a lot of stimuli and with the emotional charge of that stimuli, it can be overwhelming. The things you want to achieve might seem so far out of reach, require so much willpower to achieve, they seem almost impossible. You want those things but you know getting there won't be as fast or as easy as a movie montage scene, and it seems tiring to even begin.

So, you stick to what you know, all the while lamenting that you don't have the self-discipline it takes to get you to where you want to be.

There's another way other people can affect our self-discipline – and that's our tendency to mirror people. Our brains respond to other people's emotions, and we can start to mirror them. It's partly why smiles and bad moods can be contagious. And even when we're only mirroring someone else's bad mood, we're more likely to indulge ourselves so that we feel better.

It's also a very human tendency to want the same things as other people and to want to fit in. So, when we see somebody else indulging themselves, then we are more likely to mirror that behavior. If you're out with a friend who drinks heavily, you're more likely to indulge in a few more drinks than you would have in the company of someone else. Most of us also tend to live well within our comfort zones. We do the things we know how to do, in the ways we know how to do them, and any big changes (sometimes even small ones) can seem daunting.

You've convinced yourself that the skills, talents and personal characteristics that you have today are the only ones you will ever have. Doing anything that requires a skill or characteristic you don't feel you have is daunting, and it seems easier to just not do it. It's only when we push outside of that zone of comfort we can really change and grow – but doing so is a huge effort. And that's because your own brain is working against you.

Self-Discipline and Your Brain

In the early days of mankind, a little self-discipline was necessary to avoid the small communities we lived in from disintegrating. Humans needed the protection of the rest of their tribe, and so controlling urges that might otherwise get them kicked out of the tribe were a necessary survival skill.

Over time, as human civilization became more complex, the need for self-discipline only grew stronger. Our brains evolved to meet this new survival need, and all humans have the capacity for willpower and impulse control. But the older, more primitive parts of our brain don't always want to cooperate. Your primitive brain, the amygdala (often called the reptilian brain) has one primary driver –to keep you safe. It doesn't distinguish between types of danger, so anything that would make you uncomfortable in any way at all is something it tries to prevent. Hence the reason it's so difficult to get outside of the comfort zone that your reptilian brain loves so much.

The reptilian brain is a necessary part of us. It keeps us alive when there's a real danger, but we need to be able to understand when it's at work and ignore it when the 'danger' it senses isn't an actual threat. So, if the reptilian brain has so much control over us, how does anyone ever achieve anything? The answer is in our pre-frontal cortex. As we evolved to be self-disciplined, this section of the brain increased in size – and in functions. Initially, it was used mainly to control our movements, but it's tasks increased to include self-control – and so did its size.

Humans have the largest prefrontal cortex of any species and it's why we have the power of self-discipline. It can help to balance out the reptilian brain, making us actually want to do the things that are difficult or uncomfortable. It helps you start those tasks and to stick to them. But the reptilian brain has been part of us for longer, and its pull can be strong. This is partly why so many of us struggle to get started with doing the things we know will get us to where we want to be. Because our evolved brain wants to achieve our potential, but the amygdala is always lurking in the background, keeping you 'safe' from yourself.

The reptilian brain isn't only responsible for keeping you stuck through fear of change. It's also the part of your brain that drives addictive behaviors and makes us crave foods high in fat, salt, and sugar, among other things.

Advertisers are very familiar with the way our reptilian brain works, it's the part of us that they frequently appeal to the most. Savvy marketers understand that appealing to our reptilian brains in the right way can bypass our self-control functions. So they use techniques such as employing attractive models. This works because we either desire the model, and equate the product with sexual desire, or we want to be like the model and have what they have. So we subconsciously link the product with being attractive.

Other techniques like implied scarcity, the promise of obtaining some kind of power (more money, higher social station, etc.) or exploiting a fear are all ways that marketers appeal to our reptilian brains. It's very effective. However, when you can identify the tools being used, it makes it easier to resist the primitive impulse to do, have, or buy what they are selling. When we resist the primitive impulse, we can use our more logical pre-frontal cortex to identify if this is something we really need to help us achieve our real goals.

Of course, applying self-discipline goes beyond resisting the urge to act on impulse. Yet, once you're aware that your reptilian brain exists, and that it can be overcome, it gets easier to resist its' influence whenever it isn't serving your higher purpose. When you feel resistance to a task, or an impulse to do something, just pause and take the time to reflect on what is driving it. This is often enough to kick your more logical and rational parts of the brain into action.

The Effective Models We Can Use

Self-discipline, and exactly what drives it, has been studied extensively by psychologists. Their findings help us to understand why and how some people seem to find it easier than others to be self-disciplined, and why we sometimes quit too easily. Of course, self-discipline is the key to success, so understanding the key to why this happens and how to prevent it is of great interest to us all.

One of the key areas of study has been around why we see a depletion in willpower over time. I'm sure you've noticed at one time or another when you've been trying to apply self-discipline, it becomes oh so much harder as the day goes on.

The Metabolic Model
One of the key theories is the energy or metabolic model. According to this model, the brain has a limited amount of 'self-discipline' energy, and this reserve of energy is depleted each time we exert self-discipline. This model suggests that when we are less self-disciplined, it's down to fatigue. So, to give yourself the best chance of being self-disciplined, you need to refuel. And according to experts and studies of the time, the best way to refuel was with simple carbohydrates.

The carbohydrate theory, however, assumes that exerting self-control lowers blood glucose levels, and topping them back up replenishes willpower. However, more recent studies have challenged the way the original studies monitored this. In the new studies, while they observed the expected 'fatigue' in terms of reduced willpower, there was no drop in blood sugar after completing tasks requiring willpower.

Yet, rinsing out the mouth with a sugary solution did improve willpower. The researchers concluded that the promise of a reward or pleasurable experience (in this case, sugar) is what actually motivates you and replenishes willpower – not the metabolic blood sugar effect itself. While it's a little disappointing that a candy bar isn't the magic solution to all your willpower problems, it is helpful for those who would like to follow a healthy eating lifestyle. An excess of simple carbohydrates, especially sugar, are linked to poor health and diabetes. And that's not to mention the cavities!

Of course, complex carbohydrates (foods with a high GI), which release slowly over the day, are part of a healthy diet and give a nice stable blood sugar level. This is the best kind of fuel to help keep those energy levels, self-discipline one or other, on an even keel. So next time you find yourself lacking in self-discipline, try eating a healthy meal containing complex carbohydrates like oats or wholemeal bread. Then get to work on that task, knowing you're fueled correctly to give it your best shot!

<u>The Motivational Model</u>
The motivational model takes into account the numerous studies showing that it is more than just our blood sugar levels that impacts our self-discipline. Incentives, individual perceptions of task difficulty, personal beliefs about willpower, feedback on task performance, and changes in mood all seem to influence our willpower.

Whereas the metabolic model treats willpower almost like a muscle that needs food for fuel, the motivational model suggests that motivation is what 'feeds' your willpower. So, if you don't have the self-discipline to complete a task, or start a new habit, then you simply aren't motivated enough. Motivation is a complex beast and is very closely linked to goals – which we'll explore in-depth in a later chapter. If you don't know what you're getting out doing the task or haven't framed it in a desirable enough way, then you won't find it easy to summon the willpower.

For example, you might want to run a marathon but find that you can't summon the willpower to train for it. In this case, it's possible your reasons for running the marathon aren't motivating enough for you. To find the willpower, you must find a strong motivation.

The Process Model
This model views self-control as a process that involves both motivation and attention. The idea is that using willpower will later lead an individual's motivation to move away from impulse control and move towards gratification or rewards.

For example, being self-disciplined by avoiding unhealthy foods early in the day may cause a motivational shift where we are able to justify indulging in an unhealthy treat later on. Rather than this being caused by 'running out' of willpower, the process model posits that we simply choose to stop being self-disciplined. Our attention and focus shifts from control to gratification. As part of the shift, we stop focusing on the fact that unhealthy food is linked to lifestyle diseases like type two diabetes and obesity. Instead, we focus our attention on the idea that unhealthy food is a reward – one we now deserve for our earlier display of self-discipline.

Psychologists continue to study the various ways in which we display, or fail to display, self-discipline and self-control. Hopefully, in the future, we will learn of further breakthroughs that make self-discipline easier to understand and maintain. Until then, the information we already have allows us to put in place tools and techniques for becoming more self-disciplined.

What Happens When You Lack Self-Discipline?
A lack of self-discipline can manifest itself in many ways, none of them positive.

One obvious issue is excessive procrastination. Procrastination itself is normally down to resistance to a task. Perhaps it's boring, perhaps you're afraid to fail. You may even be afraid to succeed. Without self-discipline, we can't make ourselves just get on with the task and work through whatever is blocking us from doing it. So not only do we put things off, we delay the opportunity to learn more about ourselves. Not being able to apply self-discipline can also leave you with low self-esteem. You may consider yourself lazy, worthless, or stupid for not having the self-discipline to get things done. When you lack self-discipline, you achieve much less and may feel like you are not able to reach your goals.

Lack of self-discipline can also drive numerous unhealthy behaviors – we use self-discipline to prevent ourselves indulging in unhealthy, addictive behaviors. Without it, we're more likely to overeat, gamble, and make poor financial decisions like impulse spending. For some, it can even lead to alcoholism and abuse of drugs or other substances. If you recognize any of these behaviors in yourself, the great news is, it's not too late to change and turn it all around.

Real Life Case Study – Justin

Justin never developed his self-discipline. He didn't work hard at school and graduated with low grades. He didn't go to college and fell into a range of low-paying, low-skilled jobs. By the time he was 25, most of his old high school friends were climbing career ladders, and some had started to settle down and begin families. Justin felt stuck, and his mood was low. He didn't like where he was – his job, his rented room in a shared apartment. He wanted more from his life. Yet he didn't feel worthy of more. He resisted finding a partner, believing he had nothing to offer them. He began drinking every evening, seeking solace in the numbing effect of alcohol.

One evening, after yet another six-pack of beers, he struck up a conversation with his roommate about the secrets of success. His roommate shared that his brother was a very successful businessman, and very self-disciplined. Justin remarked that it must be nice to have self-discipline as a natural trait, and his roommate laughed. He went on to explain that his brother had been a college dropout, and his parents had worried he would never pull himself together. It wasn't until he had started to take an interest in how successful people got to where they were that he realized the truth. Not only was self-discipline the key – it was something anyone could develop.

Justin was intrigued, and the next day he started to research self-discipline. As his roommate had said, he discovered it was a skill he could develop, and he made the decision to develop it as a skill himself. He was particularly intrigued by the psychology behind self-discipline and decided to put the theories to the test. He would set a goal each week, and if he reached it, he would reward himself. His first goal was to cut back on his drinking. After a week of complete sobriety, he rewarded himself with a book on self-discipline, purchased with the money he'd saved by not drinking.

Each time he set a goal, he promised himself a reward, and each time he found he was able to achieve the goal. There were times he faltered, but he knew from his research that this would be the case and he simply resolved to continue, regardless. The more he exercised his willpower, the more it grew – and along with it his self-esteem. Over time, he built up to bigger goals until he eventually enrolled in night classes to complete a college degree – in psychology. Completing his degree required a level of self-discipline he had previously believed he didn't have, but he did complete it. After graduating, he was also able to land his dream job as a researcher, where he eventually met his future wife.

Justin's story is a great example of how applying self-discipline can change your life. Interestingly, a lot of Justin's issues stemmed from the fact that he believed he wasn't self-disciplined and had a negative self-image. Because he believed that to be true, it was his reality. When he finally learned he could break out of that reality by changing how he saw himself, he was able to make huge, positive changes to his self-discipline and his life.

In Chapter Two, we'll take a closer look at how your attitudes and beliefs can impact your self-discipline and your life.

Chapter 2 : This Can Change Everything

"Respect your efforts, respect yourself. Self-respect leads to self-discipline. When you have both firmly under your belt, that's real power."
Clint Eastwood

<u>How Attitudes and Beliefs Affect Self-Discipline</u>
From the moment you are born, you are learning. As children and teenagers, our brains are like sponges, soaking up information from every possible source. It's common knowledge that the academic education you receive has an impact on your career choices and success. It may surprise you to know, however, that it's often the other things you learn that can make or break how successful you are. As children, we're also developing a whole set of beliefs about ourselves, our abilities, and our capacity to learn, develop and achieve. We carry these beliefs with us into adulthood, and they make up our mindset.

It's becoming increasingly recognized that your mindset is the true key to your success. With the right mindset, a lack of academic qualifications is no barrier to success. A positive mindset will help you either thrive in your chosen career without paper qualifications, or it will give you all the tools to achieve any essential qualifications. A positive mindset can also boost your self-discipline. When your outlook aligns with your goals, you can achieve anything you put your mind to. What you believe becomes your reality, and when you believe that you can achieve your goals, it becomes much easier to work diligently towards them.

So, you know that having the right mindset is crucial, but how do you develop it? In this chapter, we'll look at how to develop a more positive mindset and the improvements you'll see as a result.

The Two Types of Mindset
Carole Dweck is a psychologist who wrote the groundbreaking book, Mindset. In it, she describes how there are two types of mindset. According to Dweck, people have either a **fixed mindset** or a **growth mindset**.

So, how do you identify which of these is your current mindset?

People with a fixed mindset believe that the intelligence, character, and abilities they have don't change and that they can't develop new ones. Failure for people with a fixed mindset is simply proof they are unable to achieve something.

People with a growth mindset believe they can grow, they are always learning, and they can learn and develop new skills and qualities throughout their lives. Failure for people with a growth mindset is simply a learning opportunity to grow from, not evidence that they are not capable of something.

A growth mindset allows you to be more resilient, and not to give up at the first hurdle - because you understand any setbacks are temporary. People with this mindset know that if you can understand what led to failure, you can also learn how to succeed. When you approach tasks with a growth mindset, you are applying a philosophy of persistence and perseverance that is the perfect foundation for self-discipline. This approach is proven to be consistent with success.

Accepting Failure
You will fail, and you will have setbacks. That statement might seem incongruous with the theme of this chapter – which is all about having a positive mindset. But it's important to stay in touch with reality.

What we're aiming for isn't a state of denial where you repeat positive affirmations endlessly and pretend nothing can ever go wrong. The aim is to expect success but to understand that failure is often a necessary part of the success. Accepting failure isn't a 'get out of jail free card,' it's simply choosing to brush off the failure and resolving to learn from it and do better. Some people will eat a bar of chocolate and then continue their weight-loss eating plan as normal. Others think 'I've ruined it' and continue to eat badly for the next three weeks while lamenting the fact that they just 'don't have the willpower.'

When that happens, each person has a choice. They can decide that they've ruined their diet and quit. Or they can identify why they ate the chocolate bar and take steps to prevent the same lapse in the future. Maybe they decide to carry healthy snacks with them, maybe they increase the volume of healthy food they eat at breakfast or lunch to prevent hunger and cravings. But by learning from the failure and not beating themselves up, they're giving themselves the power to succeed.

Don't believe me? If you've ever experienced failure, (and let's face it, who hasn't?!) you're in good company.
- JK Rowling was rejected by twelve different publishing houses for the first Harry Potter novel before she finally received an offer.
- Simon Cowell filed for bankruptcy at the age of 30, after his first two record labels folded. Today he is one of the most influential people in

pop music.
- Thomas Edison failed 1000 times when inventing the light bulb - before he finally created a prototype that worked.

All of these people took their failures in their stride and let them propel them to great success. And if you think that they're the outliers or special cases, then you'd be wrong.

What all these people had in common was a growth mindset. They knew that they could develop their skills, build on their failures, and ultimately achieve the success they craved. They just had to be willing to fail and to use the lessons from those failures to get them to where they needed to be.

Taming Negative Self-Talk with NLP Techniques

Without tackling your beliefs and working to change them, you are setting yourself up for failure. There might be times when you achieve a good level of self-discipline despite your negative beliefs about yourself. Unfortunately, this will often be short-lived if you haven't tackled your mindset. Almost inevitably, you'll experience setbacks and begin to convince yourself that you *'can't'* do something and that you don't have the willpower.

Everyone has that little voice in their mind that tells them they can't do something. It reminds you of the times you've failed before, and why that means you'll fail again. It latches onto any criticisms other people might make of you and replays them back to you – sometimes on a loop.

We all experience that voice. It's like a radio station in your head, broadcasting all of your personal fears and limiting self-beliefs back to you. The difference between people with the right mindset and those without is when you have a positive mindset, you don't listen to that voice. You learn how to change the channel to a more positive one.

If you believe that you are lazy and that you lack self-discipline, then you are lazy, and you will fail. To a large extent, you are what you believe you are. Of course, you didn't develop your mindset and beliefs in a day. They've been building up over your entire lifetime, and it's not something you can turn around in a day, or even a week or a month. Changing your mindset can be hard work. It's easy for old habits and thought patterns to slip back in, especially in times of stress.

However, you can make hugely positive steps toward change very quickly. With sustained effort, you can replace your old mindset and beliefs with newer, healthier ones. NLP offers some tools that can help you change your beliefs by changing the words you use in your self-talk.

The first step is in recognizing when you are experiencing negative self-talk. It's such a constant in many people's lives that we almost don't know when we're doing it. Make a commitment to pay close attention to your own self-talk for the next 24 hours. When you catch yourself saying anything negative, stop and reframe it in your mind.

For example, if your boss gives you an important task at work, your self-talk might be 'I don't know if I can do this to the standard he's expecting.' You can then reframe that as 'I'm going to do my best on this task – and I can ask for help if I need it.'

The more often you do this, the quicker your self-talk will start to change. While it's not reasonable to expect that you'll never experience negative thoughts, over time you'll find yourself experiencing positive thoughts by default more often.

Building Positivity by Tracking Progress
If you're aiming towards a big goal: losing a lot of weight, training for a marathon, becoming fluent in a language, etc., it can sometimes feel like an almost impossible task. Of course, this kind of negative thinking is exactly what you want to avoid. You can use visualization, affirmations and reframing to help it seem more achievable and build up some motivation to bolster your willpower. However, sometimes we need a little extra boost.

One way to do this is to consider the progress you have already made. It's been proven that people will work harder to achieve a goal if they can see that they have already made progress towards it. It reduces the amount of perceived effort it will take to reach your goal, and makes you more likely to follow through and put even more effort in.

If you feel that you have already made progress in some way, and you are getting closer to the finishing point, you are more likely to push forwards. To take full advantage, keep track of your goals and any and all progress, no matter how small it seems. The closer you seem to reaching your goal, the easier you will find it to put the effort in.

If you're just beginning work towards a large goal, identify any steps you might have already taken towards achieving your goal. Write a list and try to think outside of the box for this exercise. For example, if you want to lose weight, you might consider any research into effective healthy eating programs as progress towards your end goal.

Being able to see your progress can motivate you to continue with your efforts and prevent you from giving into temptation when your willpower is tested.

People With a Growth Mindset Concentrate on Effort
A key trait of people with a growth mindset is that they place as much, if not more, emphasis on the journey to a goal, and not simply the outcome. In doing this, they value the effort they put into reaching their goal more than they value the overall outcome. Of course, achieving the intended outcome is always still your goal. But by placing all of your concentration on simply achieving the outcome, you are potentially placing all the emphasis on situations that might be outside of your control.

In this instance, 'effort' also encompasses learning and growing from your failures. When following a fitness program, you might put as much physical effort into it as you possibly can, but not see results. On closer inspection, you might identify that your lack of results is down to not paying attention to proper form when completing exercises or eating the wrong type of foods which cancel out the effort put into the workout.

In this instance, you put in a lot of effort, but if you simply continue to do the same you are at risk of seeing slow or no results at best. At the worst, you risk injuring yourself or even putting weight on. So now, some of your effort needs to be applied to mastering proper form and eating a diet to maximize the results. Effort is important, but if it doesn't seem to be paying off, try new strategies and identify how you can adapt what you are doing to get you closer to your goals.

Surround Yourself With The Right Kind Of People
It's said that we become like the people we spend the most time with. Try to develop a circle of friends that are positive, successful, happy people. Surrounding yourself with people who tend to see the world negatively will influence your own outlook too. If you have very close friends and family members who are negative, and you want to spend time with them, try to be a positive influence on them. Build them up, help them see the positive in things, and they may just start to behave that way themselves.

If there are people in your life who openly reinforce your own negative self-beliefs, it's often wise to limit the amount of time you spend with them. At the very least you should have a discussion about how they can help you by not reinforcing your negative beliefs.

Fake It 'Till You Make It
Another interesting way to boost your positivity is to adopt the body language of someone who is confident and positive. It's strange, but true that by standing tall and putting on a smile, you will begin to feel happier.

In fact, a Harvard Business School professor named Amy Cuddy conducted and analyzed over 55 studies showing that adopting an expansive posture, or *'power pose'* makes you feel more powerful. Cuddy believes it can decrease the stress hormone cortisol and increase testosterone – making you feel more powerful and in control.

Try it for yourself by adopting a power pose for two minutes before any situation where you need additional self-confidence. Here are a couple of power pose examples to start with:

- **The Wonder Woman.** Stand with your feet apart, your hands on your hips, and your chin tilted upward.
- **The Performer.** Stretch your arms wide, held aloft and widen your stance. You should look like a performer soaking up the applause of an appreciative audience.

Easy Exercises To Help You Everyday

Think of a positive mindset as similar to physical health. If you take care of your body, it will perform well. If you've regularly exercised and eaten well it will stay fit and healthy for a while even if you indulge in a few bad habits. But over time, those bad habits take their toll until one day you realize you're not as fit and healthy as you used to be.

Your mindset needs regular workouts and to be 'fed' with the right things to keep it on track.
Let's take a look at some ways you can incorporate a mindset workout into your day.

Affirmations

We've already examined the need to be able to spot negative self-talk and reframe it positively. You can get even further ahead of the game by 'programming' some firmly positive beliefs into your mind using affirmations. To get the most benefit, you need to do these daily, for just a few minutes a day. Ideally, you would repeat them a few times during the day – in the morning when you get up, and before you go to sleep as a minimum.

Affirmations are easy to do, but it's vital to put some feeling into them in order to reap the benefits. You need to convince yourself that these affirmations are completely true. Of course, it can feel a little silly to repeat affirmations if you don't necessarily believe in them. It's therefore important to phrase them correctly to allow yourself to feel them and thereby incorporate them into your beliefs.

Here are some example affirmations. You can amend and adapt them to suit your own situation and make them believable for you:
- I choose to put in the time and effort needed to achieve my goals.
- I am in control of my time and my actions, and I choose to be self-disciplined.
- I keep promises to myself and others. I do what I say I am going to do.
- I have enough willpower to see any goal through to completion.
- Failures are just stepping stones to success, and I don't use them as an excuse to quit.

Choose two or three affirmations and repeat them for five minutes. Some people also like to record themselves saying the affirmations and play them back during breaks at work, or while doing household chores, etc. This way, you can hear yourself doing the affirmations even if other people are around and you would feel silly saying them out loud. This is best used as a supplement, and not entirely in lieu of speaking them aloud.

Visualizations
Another way to help your mindset is to make use of visualization. It's a tool that thousands of successful people swear by. When you visualize successful outcomes, it focuses your mind on what you are aiming to achieve. This mental image can help you dig deep and find willpower when you feel like quitting. Visualize yourself taking any

necessary actions towards your goal. Paint a vivid picture in your mind of the sense of satisfaction and any tangible benefits you'll have once the job is done.

The key with visualization is to make it as vivid and detailed as possible. For example, if your goal is to learn Italian and visit Rome, imagine your first day in Italy. Imagine yourself ordering your favorite Italian meal and making small talk with the waiter. It should be so vivid that you can almost taste the food and hear the animated chatter of other Italian dinners around you. Visualize arriving at your hotel and being able to understand all of the informational notices, asking locals for directions to the tourist attractions, etc. How will it feel when you're conversing confidently in Italian?

Another kind of visualization to try when you're experiencing a lot of negative self-talk is to imagine what someone who loves you would say. Family and friends often see the best in us, while we tend to fixate on the negative. Visualizing how a supportive friend or family member might see the situation can help you quiet the negative self-talk and replace it with more positive sentiments. Again, make it vivid and as realistic as possible. Imagine your friend or family member speaking the words in their voice and the mannerisms that accompany it.

The more you practice visualization the easier it becomes. Aim for once per day, and don't be afraid to embellish and think big! It's the perfect exercise to do when you're in bed, as it will also help you to wind down before you fall asleep, perhaps even carrying over into your dreams, making it feel like reality.

Real Life Case Study – Sarah

Sarah had worked for the same company for six years and felt stuck in a rut. She dreamed of achieving a promotion to management level, but she wasn't putting herself forward for opportunities. She believed she didn't 'have what it takes' to get a promotion. There was a certain amount of history to this belief. After her first three years with the company, Sarah had applied for a promotion and didn't get it. Her line manager gave her detailed feedback, which Sarah recognized as fair, but she didn't know how she could improve. Her manager suggested that she take on some additional projects to build her skills, but Sarah was afraid that she might not be good enough at them.

When she looked at her colleagues who achieved promotions, she felt that she wasn't like them. She convinced herself that those people had managerial skills that she didn't and that they were naturally more productive and self-disciplined. Listening to her own negative self-talk made her miserable at work, and her productivity was affected. She was putting in minimal effort and knew she needed to work harder. Yet, she couldn't seem to muster the self-discipline to excel at work.

As part of an employee well-being program, Sarah attended a compulsory workshop on how to develop a growth mindset. When the group looked at what constitutes a fixed mindset, Sarah recognized many of these traits in herself. She could see how her own fixed mindset had prevented her from using her failed application as a learning opportunity, and instead had allowed it to convince her that she wasn't capable.

Now she understood how her own negative self-talk and fear of failure was holding her back, she resolved to do something about it. Understanding the issue and how to address it was exactly the motivation boost she needed. She began by reframing her negative self-talk and working on her fear of failure. Each morning she practiced affirmations as she dressed, and each evening she visualized herself in the managerial position she wanted.

She started to switch her focus from achieving one specific outcome to valuing the effort she put in, and the learning opportunities each task presented. She revisited the feedback she'd received three years ago and worked with her manager on tracking her progress towards being ready for a managerial role. When a management position became available, Sarah applied. This time, she got an interview. Before her interview, she adopted a power pose for two minutes, helping to increase her self-confidence and repel any self-doubts and negative self-talk from sabotaging her efforts.

This time, Sarah was successful. Not only had her new growth mindset helped her to be confident enough to apply, but being able to talk about her failures and what she'd learned from them had impressed her interviewers immensely. As a new manager, she vowed to make sure that all her team had the chance to attend the same mindset workshop that had turned her career around.

In this chapter we've identified what a positive mindset looks like, and how to create one. By following the tips and techniques in this chapter, you should be able to determine when your negative self-beliefs are threatening your attempts at self-discipline and be able to start to turn the situation around.

In summary:

- Recognize failure as a learning experience – and learn from it
- Watch out for negative self-talk and reframe it positively
- Concentrate on effort over outcomes
- Practice affirmations and visualization daily to exercise that mindset muscle

It's essential to support a positive mindset by looking after your body and allowing yourself time for self-care. Without adequate self-care, focusing on self-discipline can fast become a road to burnout and exhaustion. In the next chapter, we'll take a look at how to take care of yourself in order to become more self-disciplined.

Chapter 3 : Easy To Follow Steps To Become Stronger

"Stress is an important dragon to slay - or at least tame - in your life."
Marilu Henner

Self-Nurturing For Better Self-Discipline
We've looked at how you need to pay attention to your mindset, but just as important is taking care of your body. Self-discipline is more than just setting your mind to a task, you'll need your body to comply as well. Psychologists studying self-discipline are coming to accept that our willpower can be heavily affected by diet, lack of sleep, lack of exercise, and inadequate relaxation.

When people think of self-discipline, they often imagine following a harsh regime as you might experience in a military boot camp. It conjures up images of very early mornings, cold showers, long runs in bad weather and all manner of other unpleasant but ultimately rewarding activities.

What very rarely gets acknowledged is that this is an almost impossible state to maintain, and certainly isn't necessary. There are a lot of lessons to learn about self-discipline from the military – so much, in fact, that we'll cover it in its own chapter. But normal, day-to-day, long-term self-discipline relies on a backbone of self-care and not hardcore self-denial.

Looking after yourself is an essential part of a self-disciplined life, and it's certainly not a luxury. A self-disciplined life requires you to draw on a well of strength and willpower that will run dry without adequate self-care.

Dealing With Stress

The scourge of modern lifestyles, stress needs to be managed carefully. If you're stressed or depressed, you will find it very difficult to apply self-discipline consistently. It's important to note that stress is a necessary part of life, and in fact, a little 'good' stress is what keeps us going. When we refer to 'stress,' most of us mean the bad type of stress. Sometimes these are categorized into eustress and distress

Eustress is 'positive' stress. It's what you feel when you get butterflies before public speaking or an interview. It's the feeling of anticipation and excitement that we experience when we're facing a positive challenge or experience like marriage. Overall, this is a good and necessary thing, but if you are experiencing too much of it, it can still impact you negatively.

Distress is negative stress, and as the name implies, it isn't a helpful kind of stress. It's the kind of stress that arises from experiences like bereavement, unemployment, and divorce. It can also arise from smaller issues such as dealing with challenging colleagues, high-pressure deadlines or mounting bills. Distress tends to always be unhelpful for maintaining willpower and self-discipline. We can't avoid all stress of either kind, but we can look out for the signs and symptoms that we are reaching our personal threshold for stress. Everyone's personal threshold is different, but the signs and symptoms are generally consistent. Not everyone experiences all of these, but they're a sure sign that you need to start taking better care of yourself.

Signs of stress:
- Low energy
- Headaches and/or stomach upsets
- Insomnia
- Inability to focus
- Acting impulsively

We all experience a little stress sometimes, but we often don't notice it until the symptoms are almost uncontrollable. Pay attention to how you feel each day, and it will help you notice manage fluctuating stress levels.

Make Time for Relaxation to Prevent Stress
Relaxation is a vital part of stress management. Relaxation can help to both prevent stress and to reduce it if you're already feeling the effects. Studies have shown that making time for daily relaxation keeps your stress levels lower and increases your self-control when faced with challenges to your willpower. Of course, how you choose to relax has an impact. Relaxing with an alcoholic drink and binge-watching Netflix might make you feel better in the short term, but it's unlikely to give you the positive affects you want long term.

The best and most effective way to relax is to incorporate meditation into your daily schedule. By taking the time to sit quietly and focus on your breathing, you will experience the kind of relaxation that is sometimes referred to as 'the physiological relaxation response.' This kind of relaxation slows your heart rate and breathing, and relaxes your muscles. When your mind is still, and you aren't analyzing or planning anything, your body can start to let go of the stress it's carrying.

Taking just ten minutes for meditation each day can have a profound effect on your stress levels – and in turn, help increase your ability for self-discipline.

The Magical Power of Sleep
Sleep is vital for your wellbeing, but according to a 2008 study by the National Sleep Foundation, the average amount of sleep an American adult gets is two hours less than it was in 1960. When you consider that adequate sleep is vital for self-discipline and health, it's a scary statistic. This chronic lack of sleep has also been cited by some researchers as one of the reasons for the rise in obesity in the same time period.

One reason for this could be that getting less than six hours of shut-eye a night impairs your impulse control. In fact, sleep deprivation has similar effects to being mildly intoxicated, and that's definitely not a good thing for your self-control. If you're regularly getting less than adequate sleep, your prefrontal cortex becomes temporarily impaired, making it much harder to resist the impulses of your lizard brain. Your body starts to react to normal everyday stressors in a primitive fight-or-flight manner because your lizard brain is in the driving seat. Your cortisol levels rise, and your willpower depletes rapidly.

Luckily, these effects are only temporary, and once your body is rested with a good night's sleep, your pre-frontal cortex is restored to full function again. Of course, each time you don't get adequate sleep, you'll experience these effects again. If you want to develop your self-discipline, it's time to start making sleep a priority.

For many of us, just being aware of the problem and making sure we get to bed early instead of watching movie marathons or mindlessly scrolling social media will solve the issue. However, if you belong to the 1 in 4 of us who struggle to sleep on a regular basis, try implementing some of the following tips into your evening routine:

Limit Screen Time Before Bed
The blue light that screens emit can interfere with your sleep cycle. We evolved to produce melatonin, a hormone that helps us sleep and our bodies produce it based on how much light we are exposed to. The blue light from screens disrupts melatonin production, fooling our bodies into thinking it's still daylight. Try disconnecting from all screens for an hour or two before bed. It's the perfect time to work in some meditation, take a long bath, and do some reading or journaling to wind down.

Make Sure Your Bedroom Is Dark
Even a little bit of light can disturb your sleep, including the standby lights from electrical items. Wherever possible switch electrical devices off completely or move them so that the light isn't visible. If your bedroom is rarely dark while sleeping – perhaps you work shifts, or street lamps are located close to your property - then invest in some blackout curtains. If you leave your cell phone by your bed when you sleep, turn it over so that any notifications that light the screen don't disturb you.

Avoid Alcohol
A little 'nightcap' can help you drift off quicker, but it reduces the amount of restorative REM *(Rapid Eye Movement)* sleep that you get. So, you technically might get more hours with your eyes closed, but you're not getting the full benefit of those hours. That's partly why you feel so tired after a night on the booze even if you get to bed at a reasonable hour.

Naps

If you can work them into your day, naps can be a great way to recharge your willpower batteries. They also have the added benefit of boosting focus and creativity – if you sleep for one full cycle.

It's important to have the right kind of nap to get the most benefits out of it. Get it wrong, and you might be waking mid-way through a sleep cycle. That can leave you feeling tired, groggy and disoriented for an hour or so after waking. The ideal nap leaves you rested, refreshed and ready to tackle the rest of the day.

The three types of nap are:
- **Short power nap** – sleeping for 20 minutes can give you a boost of energy and relieve fatigue.
- **Recovery nap** – sleeping for 45 minutes gives an even bigger boost of energy, as you experience both light and deep sleep – but don't sleep long enough to enter REM sleep.
- **Full sleep cycle nap** – sleeping for 90 minutes gives you the restorative benefits of one full sleep cycle. It can boost creativity as well as energy and is the best choice to combat an inadequate night's sleep.

The timings here are approximate – not everyone's sleep cycles are the exact same length, and not everyone falls asleep the minute they shut their eyes. This can make setting the alarm for the right time to wake up a little tricky. It's really important that you don't wake up at the wrong point of a sleep cycle, or you will likely feel worse than before the nap.

There are solutions to this problem. To help you get the most out of your nap, the majority of modern smartphones have an accelerometer inside them. The accelerometer can be used by special 'nap apps' to detect how much you are moving. These will wake you at the appropriate point in your sleep cycle – meaning you get all the benefits of a nap with no grogginess. Some smartwatches also have the accelerometer and the appropriate apps, and others can even use your heart rate to monitor your sleep stage and wake you at the appropriate time.

Dealing with Diet & Exercise

Diet is one of the most common areas where people struggle with self-discipline. In our modern world, convenience foods laden with sugar, salt and fats are often quicker and easier than cooking from scratch or choosing healthy foods. But it's a vicious circle. A poor diet impacts your self-discipline, and low self-discipline impacts your ability to make healthy choices. It's a chicken and egg kind of conundrum: which comes first, the self-discipline or the diet?

Eating properly is one of the best things you can do for your body and your mind. We discussed earlier how scientists believe that your blood sugar levels may be linked to your willpower. It's also widely accepted that a healthy diet with the right ratio of complex carbohydrates, healthy fats, and lean protein is crucial for a healthy body and mind. Poor diet is linked with many health issues from diabetes to heart disease and even cancer. If looking slimmer and feeling more energetic isn't reason enough, then perhaps avoiding those health issues will be the motivation you need to get started.

One of the reasons it's so hard to follow a healthy diet is that our brain is constantly working against us. For most of human evolution, we weren't surrounded by easy food sources. Our bodies would relish the chance to lay down fat stores to sustain us through lean winters, and sugary foods like fruit and naturally fatty foods like nuts would give us energy – so our bodies were designed to enjoy them. The kind of sugary and fatty foods readily available to us in nature is very different from the processed foods available on supermarket shelves.

Unfortunately, now that we can grab a highly processed candy bar as easily as an apple, we're becoming addicted to the sugary, salty foods. The issue is compounded by modern food manufacturing – often the foods we eat are heavily processed and full of substances that preserve shelf life and make us crave them. Foods as innocuous as bread can contain lots of added salt and sugar and even trans-fats that have been proven to cause health issues.

Diet doesn't have to be daunting, however. And eating for health doesn't have to involve complicated calorie counts. If you want to lose weight, making the shift first to 'clean' eating will help you make good choices when you start a calorie-controlled diet. Not all calories are created equal regarding nutrient density, and your aim should always be to pack as much nutrition into each bite as possible.

Things that can help you maintain your healthy eating:
- Eat at regular intervals. If you're not hungry, you're less likely to give in to temptation, and stable glucose levels help you maintain willpower.
- Make sure at least half your plate at each main meal is non-starchy vegetables. A healthy protein source, and whole grains or starchy vegetables should make up the other half.
- Carry healthy snacks like nuts, fruit, etc. to avoid temptation when you're hungry.
- Prepare meals in advance where possible. Crock pots are great options for making healthy cooking simple and convenient.
- Don't go grocery shopping when you're hungry and don't buy unhealthy foods. If they aren't in the house, you don't have to exert willpower when you want a candy bar.

Exercise

Alongside diet, exercise is one of the most important things you can do for your mind and your body. In fact, it could be argued that it's even more important than diet. Combine the two, however, and you have an almost magic formula for health and self-discipline.

That might sound far-fetched, but the scientific evidence of the benefits of exercise is almost indisputable.

Unfortunately, like diet, sticking to an exercise plan also requires you to have a little self-discipline. Fortunately, exercise is so effective at ratcheting up your willpower levels that if you stick to a program for more than a month, you're very likely to continue. This willpower effect will also rub off onto other areas of your life. People who exercise regularly also consume less alcohol, take fewer risks and eat healthier.

It's no coincidence that most of the world's top CEOs and successful people follow an exercise regime religiously – and it's not just to look good, although that's a pretty nice perk. So why don't more of us do it?

Some of the key reasons people give for not exercising are:
- Too busy
- Too tired
- Not fit enough
- Can't afford a gym membership or equipment
- Injury or health restrictions
- Don't enjoy it

Most of these can be overcome. If you think you're too tired or not fit enough, then these are the worst possible excuses to not exercise. You'll never be fit if you avoid all exercise! Almost everyone can manage some form of exercise – even if you start with regular short walks and build up slowly, you can definitely take steps to be more active. And exercise boosts energy, so in the long run, you'll be less tired for having incorporated exercise into your life.

If you think you're too busy, then consider that just fifteen minutes of activity a day can make a positive difference. If you can find fifteen minutes to devote to a high-intensity activity, you'll be reaping the rewards in no time. And when the benefits of exercise like sharpened focus kick in, you'll find that you power through tasks faster giving you more time to exercise, meditate, and practice proper self-care. Don't let 'busy' be your excuse.

The big exercise myth is that it depletes energy and time – when in reality it increases them. If you need a quick fix, getting outside and doing physical activity for as little as five minutes can give your willpower a big boost. According to studies, outdoor exercise enhances your self-discipline and boosts your focus as well as improving your mood and lowering stress,

This is great news for anyone who hates the idea of the gym, or a long, strenuous workout. Just five minutes of low-intensity exercise like walking or even a spot of gardening provides all these benefits. The only catch is that to get all the benefits, it does need to be in a 'green' area. A walk around a built-up city area just doesn't have the same effect, so head to your garden or the nearest park to reap the benefits.

Of course, a more rigorous exercise routine has additional benefits such as staving off lifestyle-related diseases, and depending on the program you follow, improves strength and flexibility. Joining a gym is one of the best ways to gain access to all the equipment and advice you need. If that's out of your budget, however, there are lots of effective programs that use your own bodyweight and minimal space to help you get fit.

Another option is to join a team sport. Being part of a team can help keep you motivated, and the idea you're letting your teammates down if you quit keeps you exercising even when you'd rather be at home on the sofa. Team sports are also a lot of fun and are a wonderful way to make new friends.

To reap the rewards, exercise must become a habit, so choose something you enjoy and commit to a minimum amount of time you will spend on that activity each week. If you don't think there's anything you enjoy then commit to experimenting with different types of exercise. You might hate running but love lifting weights or swimming. If you don't try them out, you'll never know.

Exercise isn't a quick-fix solution, but to develop self-discipline you need to get out of the modern quick-fix mindset. Once you see and experience your body growing stronger after several months of effort, you'll begin to see how consistent effort in other areas can build up to huge changes over time. And those changes are always more sustainable than any 'quick fix' solutions.

Don't forget to consult your doctor before starting any rigorous exercise program, and always take care to maintain the proper form for all exercises.

Real Life Case Study – Nikhil

Nikhil, a busy IT executive, found himself feeling stressed and burned out after working on a large infrastructure project for a multi-national corporation. The project was on a tight schedule and very demanding. To keep up, he'd gotten in the habit of working late nights and skipping the gym to spend more hours on the project.

After a very long day working, 'relaxing' with alcohol and take-out became the norm. His waistline expanded and his sleep became erratic. Still, he prided himself on the 'self-discipline' he was showing by putting all of his energy into the project. In the early days, it worked, and he found that he was keeping on top of the schedule. Unfortunately, as time went on, he found that he was often tired and feeling unwell, which led to him making mistakes. Correcting those mistakes took additional time, and soon he wasn't sure where he was going to find the time from to stay on schedule.

He was so tired that his work ethic began to suffer, and sometimes instead of the late nights working he was watching movies all night. The next day, he'd feel guilty for his lack of willpower, and work through lunch to try and make up for it. He complained to his colleague that all his initial hard work wasn't paying off, and his colleague suggested spending less time working on the project and more time working on himself. Nikhil was aghast. How would he catch up spending less time working? No, what he needed was more self-discipline and the focus to work harder.

His colleague pointed out that it would be stupid to expect a car to run with an empty tank so why was he expecting it of himself? Nikhil was still skeptical but agreed to implement his colleague's advice.

Despite feeling tired and unwilling, he scheduled 30-minute sessions at the gym each morning, marking them a non-negotiable. Each evening, he closed his laptop at 7.30pm at the latest and cooked a meal made of natural, unprocessed foods. An hour before bed, he made time for meditation and reading.

Despite his initial reluctance, he found that his focus improved quite quickly. He woke refreshed each morning, and his mind felt sharper after visiting the gym each morning. Before his first week was up, the reluctance he felt initially at attending a gym session every day had been replaced with positive anticipation. And after working hard at the gym, takeout seemed less appealing each evening than eating healthy, nourishing foods.

He was better able to concentrate during his workday, and not only did he make fewer mistakes, but he also completed more work in less time than he had previously. Despite devoting a few hours less each day to the project, he was keeping to the schedule and providing better work. Alongside the work-related benefits, he also noticed that he felt healthier, looked slimmer, and had more energy.

If you're burning the candle at both ends like Nikhil was, implementing the tips in this chapter will help you not only with your self-discipline but also with your overall health and wellbeing. Implementing these will require a little self-discipline on your part – but by investing a little self-discipline, you'll soon be harvesting a whole lot of willpower!

That extra willpower will give you the boost you need to reach your goals. In Chapter 4, we'll be looking closely at goals: how to set goals that are both challenging and achievable, and how to sustain your motivation to achieve them.

Chapter 4 : Easily Set Goals & Motivators

"People with goals succeed because they know where they're going."
Earl Nightingale

Chances are, if you're reading this book, then you have goals. That is, you have something you wish to achieve, and you believe you will need the self-discipline to get you there. Simply having goals can make you more successful and keeping them in mind boosts your self-discipline. Willpower feeds on the anticipation of success.

But do you *really* know what your goals are?

It's surprising how few people are completely tuned in to what they want to achieve in life – and why they want to achieve it. But when you get clear on your goals, amazing things can happen.

The True Power Of Goals
Everybody wants to know the secrets to success, and it seems like every other week there's a new 'secret' revealed. 5 am early morning starts, making your bed daily, exercising, meditating, these are all things that have been touted as the ultimate key to being successful in life. While there's a small amount of evidence for some of them, there's one clear key that crops up in study after study:

Having clear goals is **crucial** to achieving success.

It makes perfect sense when you consider it. How do you know the way to get somewhere, when you don't know where *'somewhere'* is? Sure, you might get lucky without having a destination in mind, but why rely on luck?

But merely having the goals isn't really enough to ensure that you'll have the willpower to see them through. It puts you ahead of the race in terms of success, but it's by no means a guarantee you'll get there. Luckily, there's plenty you can do to improve your chances of success, and we'll take a look at them in this chapter.

Its Important To Know Why You Want To Achieve Your Goals

A key component of consistently achieving your goals is understanding why you want to achieve them. A thorough understanding of what drives you towards the goals and how your life will be better when you achieve them will help drive your motivation levels through the roof! As Frederick Nietzsche famously said, *'He who has a why can endure any how.'*

Your WHY is the purpose, cause or belief that drives you toward your goals. Here's a short exercise to help you gain clarity on your why:

The Toddler Test

Write down your goal – for example, to learn Mandarin Chinese.

Now answer the question, *"why?"* Write down the first thing that occurs to you, no matter how silly it may seem. Your answer might be: *"So I can improve my career prospects."* Easy, right? But we're not done.

Now, ask yourself why again. Why would learning Mandarin Chinese improve your career prospects? *"So I can work with global businesses."*

You know what to do now, right? Ask yourself why again. What difference would working with global businesses make to you? *"Because I want a career that involves overseas travel."*

Why? *"Because I want to experience different cultures."*

Why? *"Because it will enable me to grow as a person, and also be paid for doing something that I find fulfilling."*

I like to call this the toddler test. Just keep asking why, until you get to the very bottom of things. Don't accept the first response, unleash your inner toddler and ask *'why?'* until it can't possibly be asked anymore.

Your own examples may have many more, or far fewer, 'why's' to get you to the bottom of what drives you towards that particular goal. Don't forget there are no right or wrong answers, just don't stop asking why until you've uncovered your real motivations.

Choose Your Top 3
It's possible that you have numerous goals, but focusing on too many at a time can fragment your focus and make it less likely that you'll achieve any of them.

In the previous exercise, you identified why achieving your goals would make a positive difference to you. Based on this, you need to choose the top 3 goals that you want to focus on. Before you do so, look to see if any of your goals are linked. If one goal naturally leads to another – like running a marathon and getting fit – then they are conceivably part of the same goal. One is the overall goal, and the other is a sub-goal – a step towards the final outcome.

An easy way to do this is to separate your goals into career, family/home life, and personal development. List each goal under one of these columns, and then order each column by priority.

There's bound to be a little overlap, so just put each goal in the column it fits into best based on your own logic. For example, *'getting a flexible job'* might go into family life because you want the flexibility to improve quality time with your family. Or, it might go into the career column because it involves getting a new job. As long as each column has a few options in it, it doesn't matter too much which column each goal is in.

Now prioritize each column by identifying how much impact achieving the goal would have on your life and how easy it is to achieve regarding time or other resources. Any that are high impact, low-medium resource should be the first things you concentrate on. Pay attention to complimentary goals too, where one goal isn't a natural 'step,' but helps in some way towards achieving another, and concentrate on those together.

Now that you have your top 3 goals, these should be your absolute priority. At the end of each week, get into the habit of asking yourself how much of your time was spent moving you towards those goals? If it wasn't most of your time, then you'll need to work on increasing it.

The Right Way To Set Goals – And Stick To Them!

So now you know, in essence, what your goals are. The next step is to frame and record them in the right way, and break them down into achievable steps. Doing this serves several purposes:

1. It makes you accountable. You've written them down and set a deadline, and that makes you 42% more likely to achieve them already based on a study by the Dominican University in California.
2. Breaking them down into steps makes the big goals seem less out of reach, and gives you a clear path forward to achieve them. If you can see exactly how your goal can be achieved, it's easier to find the willpower to push through if you hit a snag or have a bad day.
3. Recording your goals in the right way means that you know exactly what you're aiming for, and how long it will take you to achieve them.

The *'gold standard'* for goal frameworks is **SMART**. *Specific, Measurable, Achievable, Relevant, Time-Bound.* Take each of your big life goals and make sure they fit the SMART framework – then break them down into smaller goals using the same framework.

Specific: There's a world of difference between 'I want to run a marathon' and 'I want to run the New York Marathon next year in under 4 hours.' One is a vague goal that can be pushed back indefinitely and allows you to make excuses: you will do it one day, just not yet. The second is a very specific goal that will spur you to action in order to avoid failing to achieve it.

Make your goals specific and take away your reptilian brain's excuses!

Measurable: Our example goal 'Run the New York Marathon next year in under 4 hours' is a good example of a measurable goal. To achieve the goal, you need to run the marathon in under 4 hours. Most specific goals tend to be measurable by default but don't skip this one on your goal setting checklist as it's crucial for success.

Examples of unmeasurable goals are: 'get fit' and 'own a successful business.' To make them measurable, you might change them to 'reduce body fat % from 34% to 25% in six months. And 'own a business with over $100,000 net profit by the end of next year.'

Achievable: There's no point setting a goal that is going to be impossible for you to reach. Almost anything is possible with enough self-discipline and dedication, but don't set the bar so high that you can't get there. Our example of 'run this year's New York Marathon in under 4 hours' is achievable for some people. However, if you're starting with zero fitness levels, you might want to adjust the immediate goal to 'Run the New York Marathon in under 5 hours next year.' You can always have a longer-term goal of 'Run the New York Marathon in under 4 hours within the next 3 years.'

The timescales and goals are up to you to decide, but while you want them to be stretched, they shouldn't be out of reach.

Relevant: Your goals should be relevant to your lifestyle and to your other goals. A goal to 'Run this year's New York Marathon in under 4 hours' might not be relevant if your main life goals don't relate to fitness in any way. Marathon training is a heavy time investment, and if it doesn't fit with and complement your other goals, it can mean that you're stretching yourself too far.

Look at your goals holistically to make sure that they are relevant to each other, and to your overall life goals.

Time-Bound: This criterion is often taken care of by both the specific and measurable parts of the checklist. However, it's essential to set a reasonable timeframe in which each goal needs to be achieved. Without it, it's easy to let the goal slide when you don't feel like you have enough willpower to work towards it.

You don't have to set a specific day or time, but there should be a reasonable time frame involved. You couldn't learn a whole new language in two months, or go from a couch potato to a marathon runner in two weeks – so set the timeframes accordingly.

Maintaining Focus On Goals

To increase your chances of success, focus on one goal from your top 3 at a time (unless two of them are highly complementary). Choose the one that will make the most difference to you when it is achieved or the one that will be quickest to achieve.

If there's one that's both quick to achieve and makes a big impact, then that's your top priority. The willpower boost you will get when you achieve it will spur you on for your next goal.

Don't Fall Into The Resolution Trap
Every January 1st, millions of Americans set New Year's Resolutions. By February, 80% have already quit or failed. But aren't resolutions just goals? So, what is it about resolutions specifically that means they don't stick? Here are some key reasons:

- Resolutions rarely follow the SMART format. People tend to make resolutions like 'lose twenty pounds' with no specific timeframe, or the vague 'get fit.' Resolutions like 'quit smoking' are slightly less vague, but with no detailed measure of success they are still not set up to be successful.

- People rarely focus on the 'why' of the resolution. They choose something to improve and resolve to improve it. But it's essential to do a thorough examination of exactly why you want to achieve this goal, and what a successful outcome will look and feel like to you. With a clear 'why' you're much more likely to follow through and achieve it.

- Resolutions tend to only be short-term. As they are a yearly phenomenon, you'll normally only be making resolutions that can be achieved within a year. They rarely take your big picture goals into account – meaning that you'll lose motivation quickly when they cease fitting in with your wants.

Motivation
So how do you avoid the resolution effect, and keep up your motivation levels? It's unrealistic to expect your willpower to meet your goals to remain static. There will be good days and bad days, so how do you make sure that the former outweigh the latter?

You need the right type of motivation.

There are two basic types of motivation: *Intrinsic and Extrinsic.*
Intrinsic motivation is the motivation that comes purely from inside you. It's that feeling of determination you have when there's a challenge that you want to master.

Extrinsic motivation is a motivation that is dependent on external factors. Extrinsic motivation is often physical rewards such as money or possessions, but can also be a motivation that depends on other people such as public recognition. These things can be very motivating for a short while– but that motivation doesn't last forever.

For example, it's often assumed that money is a key motivational factor at work. Surprisingly, for the vast majority of people studies have shown that it's not their main motivator to get to work every day and do a good job.

It's not that money isn't a motivator, in fact, it's very effective in the short term. But what actually motivates most people longer-term is overcoming a challenge, mastering a skill, and basically feeling like they are working towards something meaningful.

So, external motivators aren't the amazing recipe for motivation that they might seem at first glance.

When you combine both intrinsic and extrinsic motivators, however, you see people's motivation levels increase drastically. Consider the lure of video games. They combine a challenge you want to succeed at alongside motivational rewards – level ups, badges, points, league table places. This is one of the reasons that businesses have been increasingly incorporating what they call 'gamification' to motivate their employees.

This is another reason knowing why your goals matter, is important – it drives motivation. Remembering exactly why you're aiming for something – what makes it meaningful to you - can give you that extra daily boost to work towards it when temptation comes knocking.

Intrinsic motivation can be broken down into three further categories: autonomy, purpose, and mastery.

Autonomy: We need to feel that we are in charge of our own lives and not simply following the rules and directions of others. While some direction is useful, in order to promote motivation, there needs to be an element of autonomy – the freedom to complete a task in your own way.

People managers often tap into this type of motivation by delegating tasks by outcome. Instead of providing a set way to complete the task, they will simply provide the expected outcome and any non-negotiables, and leave the rest to the employee. For example, they might delegate the task of improving customer satisfaction by 5% within an allowed budget but then leave the decision of how to achieve this down to the employee.

Mastery: We want to be good at things. We tend to enjoy things we excel at, and quite often it's the fact we're good at them that provides the enjoyment and not always the task itself. Writers practice and perfect their work over the years, seeking mastery.

Of course, true mastery can't be easily defined or achieved, but humans are programmed to become the very best at what they choose to do. This drive is the secret behind many successful sportspeople and businesspeople. If you only feel the urge to master your craft, then it's possible you're pursuing the wrong ones!

Purpose: We need to feel like what we're doing achieves something. It might be political change, or the drive to teach young people. When we feel like what we do has a purpose, we are much more motivated to succeed. The purpose can be anything at all; we tend to think of humanitarian and 'noble' causes when we think of purpose, but purpose can be as simple as making a difference to customer satisfaction or driving a business towards success.

If you look back at the answers to the exercise on defining your 'why,' you'll probably see that your 'why' fits into one or more of these categories.

Negative motivators: We almost always think of motivation as a positive driving force, but sometimes what is motivating us is avoidance of a negative and not the pursuit of a positive.

For example, if your income doesn't match your lifestyle, you might be motivated to take a job you don't enjoy because you want to avoid financial suffering. Or conversely, being unhappy with a job might motivate you to take a new job that you do enjoy more.

The avoidance of suffering, or negative consequences, is an external motivator and can be a powerful one, but like many other external motivators, it can also be short-lived. The threat of suffering or negative consequences has to be quite large to force us into being disciplined enough to make big changes. Negative motivators can also lead you to make hasty decisions or set 'goals' that don't really serve your bigger picture. Be aware of what motivating factors are driving your goals, and do your best to ensure that your motivations are mostly positive.

Self-discipline and motivation go hand in hand. Forcing self-discipline without having any motivation is almost impossible – and is probably closer to suffering than the empowerment of true self-discipline.

To a certain extent, what motivates you is a personal matter, but it's crucial to understand which motivations are stronger for you. Be sure to understand how reaching your goals satisfies all of your motivation types and you'll find it much easier to work up the willpower to achieve them

Real Life Case Study – Daniel

Daniel set resolutions every single year, and every year he failed to achieve them. It had become almost a running joke among his friends and family. From learning to play the guitar, to getting a second college degree, they always fell by the wayside before March.

This year, he decided to take a different approach. Instead of setting the usual vague resolutions like *'get a new job'* and *'lose weight,'* Daniel thought about his big-picture goals, and what he wanted to achieve overall. For the entire month of January, he spent the time necessary to get clear on his *'why'* and to write down his goals in a **SMART** format.

Daniel's work on his 'why' revealed that he loved drawing and creating and that he wanted a new job that used his creative talents to their full potential. Ideally, it would also earn him more money so that he could pursue his second passion of travel. His current job as a project manager just wasn't fulfilling enough.

His ultimate goal was to become an illustrator for children's books, but this would need him to complete that second degree. So he would focus on this first. Obviously, he knew this goal would need more than one year to complete. But having a proper plan in place and understanding how it would change his life gave Daniel all the motivation he needed. This time, he immediately enrolled on his degree course and found the self-discipline to attend all evening classes and work on assignments on top of his full-time job. His friends and family were amazed when he finally finished his degree and landed a well-paid internship at a large publishing house.

Daniel was able to be self-disciplined and keep up his motivation because he was clear on how each goal fit into the overall plan, and the impact a successful outcome would have on his life.

We've investigated some of the theories and science around self-discipline, and how to lay the foundations for success with SMART goal setting and visualization. It's time to move on and look at some in-depth techniques for building self-discipline that really works.

In the next part of the book, we'll be investigating how you can build consistent habits that lead to success; the lessons you can learn about self-discipline from the military; and how to avoid procrastination.

Chapter 5 : Quickly Gain Motivation & Improve Dedication To Dealing With Habits

"We are what we repeatedly do. Excellence, then, is not an act, but a habit."
Will Durant

Why Habits Are The Key To Self-Discipline
In the previous chapter, we looked at the role that motivation and willpower play in becoming self-disciplined. While those things are important, building good habits is the true bedrock of a self-disciplined life. Of course, without some motivation to start these habits, you'll never become self-disciplined at all. However, once the right habits are ingrained into your daily life, the need for motivation becomes much less.

The whole point of a habit is that it's a consistent and regular behavior. Some habits are almost automatic, and building the right ones is crucial for success. Because once you train yourself to do all the things you need to do, almost on auto-pilot, it makes self-discipline incredibly sustainable.

Why Motivation Alone Isn't Enough
Even when you tap into all the different kinds of motivation: intrinsic, extrinsic, and the various sub-categories, motivation eventually fades. It's certainly important to be motivated, but when it comes to self-discipline habit is king.

Without habit, when your motivation wanes, it becomes difficult to keep up with the disciplined actions that bring you closer to achieving your goals. You're less likely to push through anything uncomfortable and may simply give up. You won't stop wanting your goal but doing the uncomfortable work to get there will seem like too much effort.

Yet when you build powerful habits, you'll take those uncomfortable or difficult actions simply because they are a habit. For example, becoming physically fit requires consistent action. Without forming a habit of regularly exercising you could find yourself back at square one as soon as your motivation wanes. Habits are incredibly powerful. Once they are fully formed, you barely even need self-discipline to maintain them. Because habits become automatic behaviors, you need very little willpower, and your reptilian brain won't resist the actions. In fact, it will probably crave them; as your reptilian brain loves routine.

Creating habits sets you up for success. A habit of daily exercise will almost guarantee to improve your fitness levels, provided it's a good amount of exercise. Aim do some form of low-impact exercise on rest days, like a relaxing walk in nature, or gentle yoga stretches. Doing this conditions your brain to understand that this is a habit. It makes it much easier to stay disciplined and carve out the time to get the exercise done. No excuses, just action. It becomes something you do daily and that you make time for, instead of something you're just 'trying to fit in' to your day.

Creating daily habits takes away the stress of being self-disciplined. There's no decision fatigue –you're not deciding to exercise, or to write, or to study, or complete your chores. It's something you simply do without thinking about it. When your self-disciplined actions have become daily habits, they're now just actions – minimal self-discipline required.

Consider the people in your life who you believe to be very self-disciplined. What are their habits? What actions do they take daily?

It's very likely that rather than being self-disciplined machines with the willpower of steel, they simply made their uncomfortable actions habits that they do daily.

Over the long term, only the permanent change of making actions a habit can ensure your lasting success. So it makes sense to concentrate on building daily habits, one at a time, that provide a cornerstone for your self-disciplined lifestyle.

The Simple and Effective Guide To Forming Habits

So, all you have to do is make uncomfortable or difficult actions a habit, and success is yours. Except, forming a habit isn't easy. At least not the kind of habits that are good for you. So why is it relatively easy to form a bad habit like smoking or recreational drug taking, but so very difficult to build good habits like exercise or studying?

The answer, according to science, is in dopamine. We're wired to seek gratification, and most of the things that provide immediate gratification are unfortunately bad for us. Fatty, sugary foods, recreational drugs, even social media, all trigger dopamine and this make us want to have more.

Good habits like studying or exercising don't give this kind of immediate gratification. Our pre-frontal cortex knows that reaching our goals will ultimately be far more satisfying than giving in to immediate temptation. But that seems so far away for our reptilian brain that it doesn't want to concentrate on those. Not when eating that bar of chocolate, or wasting an hour on social media will give it the instant gratification it craves.

So how do you build good habits? The key is in the repetition. If you repeat a behavior enough times, it becomes a habit. Unfortunately, there's no real magic number. You might have heard it said that it takes 21 days, or perhaps 30 days to form a habit. Unfortunately, science doesn't quite back this up.

Studies have suggested that it takes anywhere from 18 to 254 days of repetition to form a new habit. So, that 21 days might not be nearly enough, depending on the habit you're trying to build. In fact, the average is 66 days. So, a little over two months on average to make something a habit. Based on this, it's a reasonable expectation that it will take at least two months of daily repetition to build a habit. So, you're going to need enough motivation and self-discipline to get you through this habit-forming stage. After the habit is built, it will become much easier to maintain it.

During this habit-forming stage, it's crucial that you stick to your plans. When you say you're going to go for a daily run, it absolutely must be daily. Nothing must stop you from achieving this goal. Not the weather, not last night's alcohol intake, nothing. Of course, some things are out of your control, but you owe it to yourself to come up with creative solutions and not give in. For example, if there's a freak snowstorm and you can't leave your home? Set a timer and run up and down your stairs, or jog on the spot instead of your normal run.

If you catch yourself making excuses to not do it, then you know it's not a habit yet. Just bear in mind that if you don't do it, you're wiping out all those days of consistent habit building and may have to start right back at square one! Trust me, although perhaps a negative motivator, this thought alone can be enough to kick your ass into action!

Using Triggers To Build And Break Habits
Triggers are events or actions that 'trigger' the habit response. For example, if you smoke, it may be that you always have a cigarette when you have a coffee. The coffee is your trigger for the habit. Triggers can be anything – people, emotions, the time of day, a location, or any action we regularly do. It's anything at all that our mind associates with a habit.

Triggers can be used in a positive way to help you build good habits. By linking the habit to a trigger, you're more likely to maintain the habit long-term and cement it in your routine as a true habit. This association is known in neuroscience as *'Hebbian Learning.'* The more often something triggers an action, the more and more ingrained it becomes as a habit, until it's pretty much just an automatic response.

Consider what triggers you have currently. Do you always have a glass of wine after a stressful day? Or eat sugary foods when you're tired? If you have habits you'd like to break, identifying the trigger can go a long way towards helping you understand how to break the habit.

Emotions can be strong triggers for habits, but as they are less consistent than activities like waking up, brushing your teeth, etc., they aren't always the best triggers for good habits. Unfortunately, we often have bad habits linked to emotional triggers, like stress eating or drinking alcohol to either unwind or to celebrate when we feel happy. If it's a trigger that can be removed completely, then that's the fastest way to break the habit.

Otherwise, consciously replacing the habit action with a new one will attach a new, healthier habit to the trigger. As we've looked at previously, you'll need to have the willpower and self-discipline to implement a different action for your trigger. However, at some time between 2 and 9 months, the new habit will become fully formed, and your bad habit will be a distant memory.

So, if you normally have a glass of wine when you get home feeling stressed – replace it with 20 minutes of exercise, or a 10-minute meditation. Instead of eating sugary food when you're tired, if you can, take a power nap instead. Or take a brisk walk to wake yourself up. Or, simply replace the sugary food with something healthier like a banana. It will still give you a little sugar boost, but is a much more nutritious choice than a peanut butter cup!

Replacing one habit with another is one thing, but how do you start a habit with a new trigger - one that doesn't have a habit attached already?

<u>Becoming Trigger Happy</u>
Write down your regular routine – the things you do every day without fail. To be a good trigger, it must be something you consistently do daily, without any conscious effort and can't be easily avoided. Then identify which of these make a good trigger for the habit you want to form.

Some examples of common triggers are:
- Waking up
- Brushing your teeth
- Showering

- Eating a meal
- Break Times
- Arriving at work
- Sitting down at your desk
- Finishing work
- Getting into your car
- Arriving home
- Cooking dinner
- Eating dinner
- Going to bed

Everybody's routines are different, and so your own potential triggers may look very different. Once you have a list of potential triggers, choose one that is the best fit for the habit you want to create.

For example, if your new habit is to keep on top of daily chores, you might choose to do the chores each day as soon as you arrive home from work. If your new habit is to meditate daily, you might choose going to bed as the trigger and complete a meditation session before going to sleep.

If you don't have an existing trigger you feel you can use, you could always set the alarm on your phone for a specific time each day. The alarm should be 'snoozed' until you've completed your new habit activity. The potential issue with this is that if the time you choose isn't convenient every single day, you might be tempted to ignore or turn off the alarm. Locations can also be a powerful trigger. It's one of the reasons that sleep hygienists regularly warn against using your bedroom for anything other than sleep and relaxation. When you associate a particular place strongly with an activity, you will encounter no resistance to doing that activity in the relevant location.

So, if you're looking to build a habit of daily study or work, choose a special location where that is the only thing you do. It could be a particular room or just a special chair. By building the association with that location and your new habit you'll find that every time you sit in your chair or enter the room, you'll be ready to complete your new habit.

Some Simple, But Powerful Habits To Start With
Creating new habits is the best way to build self-discipline, but it's important not to rush in and try to build ten or more new habits all at once. As we've seen, it can take months to build a new habit. Until it becomes a true habit, you will have to remind yourself constantly and use your willpower to complete the habit activity.

As your willpower isn't infinite, trying to create too many habits all at once is almost certain to result in you failing at some or all of them. Instead, choose one habit at a time to introduce (or replace). Once you're certain it's become a true habit, only then should you move on to introducing other habits. It's very tempting to try to do everything at once, and sometimes forcing yourself to slow down and focus on one change at a time can feel frustrating. However, slow and steady is the best way to build long-term and sustainable change.

You may have some specific habits in mind to start with, but here are some habits that are frequently associated with successful people:

Waking Up Early
Waking up as early as 5 am has frequently been associated with successful businessmen and entrepreneurs. The idea was made incredibly popular by Hal Elrod's bestselling *'The Miracle Morning.'* In the book, he discusses how

starting each morning early, and beginning the day in a particular way can get you off on the right foot and contribute to overall success.

There are plenty of positives to being an early riser. Getting up before the rest of your family can give you time in peace and quiet before starting your day. It's a great time for exercise, meditation or reading. All of these activities feature in *'The Miracle Morning.'* It's also a good time to get ahead of the day in terms of work or even complete a few chores.

The downside to the early mornings is that it doesn't always fit in with everybody's lifestyle or body clock either. Of course, there's an element of self-discipline at play here. If you normally stay up late watching movies, applying some self-discipline to get to bed earlier will make getting up early much easier. However, for people like shift workers, or parents of small children whose sleep patterns rely on outside factors and are unpredictable at best, it might not be a plausible habit to build.

Of course, you don't have to get up at the crack of dawn to gain some of the benefits. While many top CEOs and entrepreneurs cite 5 am as their preferred time to get up, simply rising an hour earlier than usual will give you some extra time to start your day off right and implement a new habit. In fact, *'The Miracle Morning'* centers around starting your day just one hour earlier. During this hour, you could dedicate some time to journaling, meditating, reading and exercising to get your day off to the best possible start.

If you do decide to become an earlier riser, don't forget to make sure that you still get adequate sleep!

Disconnecting From Social Media
Lots of us spend a lot of time on social media each day. It may not feel like much time if you only check it now and then, but those few minutes here and there can really add up.

Checking your social feeds too regularly can really mess up your productivity. It also prevents you from hitting that deep level of focus where you power through even the hardest of tasks. And too much screen time in the hours before bed can disturb your sleeping patterns, leaving you tired and less productive the next day.

It's unrealistic to say don't use social media but restricting your usage can provide some real benefits. Try to avoid checking social media as soon as you wake up, during your working hours, and for a couple of hours before bed. If you use public transport, you could designate your commute time as social media time, use your lunch break at work, or allocate some time in the early evening.

If you find this a hard habit to begin, there are special apps you can download for your phone and desktop. These will stop you from accessing social media sites for the amount of time that you specify. It's well worth the effort to implement this one. Not only will you be more productive, but you'll sleep better too.

Exercise
If you take away only one thing from this entire book, make it the importance of daily exercise.

Let's recap some of the benefits of regular exercise that we've already covered:
- It makes you automatically more self-disciplined
- It helps you sleep better

- It keeps you healthy and reduces your chances of some chronic diseases
- It improves your mood

Exercise is one of the most common activities that people want to develop self-discipline for, and the one most people struggle to fit seamlessly into their daily lives. The truth is, all of us have enough time in the day to make exercise a habit. Once we employ the willpower and self-discipline to make it a true habit, it's one that we will cherish for a lifetime.

Exercise makes you feel good. Perhaps not in the early stages if you've been completely inactive, but after only a few workouts you start to recognize that exercising is making you feel good. Endorphins kick in during a workout, and you start to see the immediate benefits to sleep and mood. Over time, your body responds, and you feel stronger, your clothes fit better, and you practically crave the exercise instead of dreading or trying to avoid it.

It can take some adjustments to your lifestyle but making exercise a true habit is one of the best things you can do for yourself.

Real Life Case Study – James

James, a chemistry student, had developed a habit of drinking twelve cans of diet soda every day. Initially, he'd switched from the sugar-laden versions, and had thought that he was replacing a bad habit with a healthier one.

However, after learning of the dangers of consuming too much caffeine and too much artificial sweetener, James began to suspect that the diet drinks were causing his frequent migraines and poor sleep. He vowed to stop drinking them and had been telling himself he would start this *'soon.'* He'd manage to cut down for a few days at a time but always ended up going back to his excessive consumption.

When his migraines and constant fatigue began to impact his grades, he decided he had to really and truly commit to breaking the bad habit. He started by identifying what his triggers were. To do this he kept a daily log of when he drank a can of diet soda, and what he was doing just before – or what he was about to start doing. He found that he had two key triggers. One was studying. Any time he was sitting down to study, he would get a can of diet soda first. He'd come to associate the soda with the studying and would grab a can without even thinking before he began any study.

The second trigger was tiredness. He'd drink a can first thing in the morning to try to shake off the groggy, just woken up feeling. Then in the evening's he'd drink more cans to try to stay awake to watch movies or play video games, thinking wrongly it was helping him to unwind.

James decided to change his habit to drinking a glass of water when the triggers occurred instead. For the first couple of weeks, he had to force himself to remember to drink water instead of soda. He stopped buying diet soda from the grocery store, but his roommate still drank it, so the temptation beckoning from the refrigerator remained. It took a conscious effort and plenty of willpower for James to not simply grab a soda first thing in the morning, or when studying. On a few occasions, he'd already opened a can before he realized and had to pour it away.

By the third and fourth weeks, he didn't need to remind himself constantly, and the action of getting a glass of water was becoming more natural. While he wasn't automatically grabbing cans of soda anymore, it still took a lot of willpower to resist having 'just one soda' when he was tired. However, the reduction in his migraine frequency and his improved sleep helped him to stay on track and concentrate his willpower.

Over the following month, it gradually became less and less difficult to resist the lure of soda, and getting a glass of water became second nature. He stopped even considering drinking soda most of the time. By the time 6 months were up, James' sleep and migraines had both drastically improved, and he had successfully reduced his diet soda intake to zero. Even better, he no longer needed to employ willpower, as the habit of drinking only water was fully formed.

We've covered some great ways to build self-discipline so far. At this point, you should know how self-discipline works, what your goals are and why they matter and be ready to start building habits that set you up for success.

In the next chapter, we'll take a look at the lessons you can learn about self-discipline from the military.

Chapter 6 : Lessons From The Unexpected

"Discipline is the soul of an army. It makes small numbers formidable; procures success to the weak, and esteem to all."
George Washington

When you think of self-discipline, there's often one institution that springs to mind: the military. Developing the skills necessary to be a good soldier requires extreme self-discipline, so where better to learn some self-discipline secrets than the military?

External Discipline vs. Self-Discipline
As we've seen, self-discipline doesn't happen overnight, but building the right habits can build your self-discipline. That's why most military recruits go through a boot camp phase. It gets them ready both physically and mentally for combat and sets them up with the right habits so that self-discipline become second nature. Of course, the military is famous for its use of external discipline in order to instill these habits so quickly and thoroughly.

External discipline is the threat of consequences. It's what holds the law together, and on a much smaller, less extreme scale it's what many parents rely on at least some of the time to get their children to cooperate.

External discipline can be anything from the threat of physical harm, to having your favorite toy taken away as a child. As long as the punishment is something you want to avoid, it will work to some extent as an external discipline.

Military Boot Camp and Self-Discipline
The point of boot camp is to get recruits to the point that the external discipline is no longer what drives the

behavior. Over time, it becomes internalized and is now self-disciplined behavior. Military boot camp looks very extreme to an outsider. But when their own lives, the lives of their comrades and the fate of an entire country could be resting on the shoulders of these recruits, it's imperative that self-discipline is learned quickly, and thoroughly.

During boot camp, every single day is about building discipline. Recruits are pushed hard beyond what they thought were their limits: both physical and mental. Failure is not an option, and excuses are not tolerated. It's a do or die mentality that's necessary to prepare them for warzones.

In these early days, the discipline is usually entirely external. Recruits are yelled at mercilessly, and face punishments for the slightest infraction. It seems harsh, but using external discipline to such extremes provides enough short-term negative motivation for the recruits to develop the right daily habits. It gives them the mental toughness needed to survive and thrive in extreme situations. The word *'impossible'* no longer seems to exist: with enough hard work and self-discipline, boot camp soldiers have learned almost anything is possible to achieve.

While you probably won't be attending a military boot camp any time soon, there are plenty of lessons you can take away and implement in your daily civilian life. The first one is taking responsibility.

Taking Responsibility
Being responsible means that you stand behind your actions and accept that your actions have consequences – for yourself, and for other people. In the military, your actions could endanger or save not just your own life, but that of your colleagues, and of innocent civilians.

Soldiers don't have the luxury of excuses or denial, they must accept responsibility for their actions. Knowing that you are accountable for your actions and the impact they have on others leads you to make more considered decisions. It also prevents you from quitting when things get tough. It promotes integrity and empowers you to take full control of your life.

Responsibility and self-discipline go hand-in-hand. When you know that achieving your goals depends entirely on you, it's impossible to fall back on old and tired excuses like 'I'll never get promoted because my boss doesn't like me.' When your excuses are removed, it's down to you to find solutions. Perhaps your boss doesn't like you, and or perhaps you're making assumptions. When you're not taking responsibility, you let your belief that your boss dislikes you become an excuse to not try.

When you accept responsibility, you find a solution. You might look at why your boss might not like you and if there are ways you can adapt your behavior to change their view. Or, you perform so well at work that it would be impossible for your boss to overlook you. Alternatively, you might find a new job and make a fresh start. Either way, the main character in control of your career is now you – not your boss. Nobody else has control of your life, and nobody else is responsible for your successes or your failures. Excuses are easy to cling to, but they keep us static. Taking responsibility feels scary and difficult, especially when deep down, we know that the biggest thing holding us back is ourselves. But it doesn't have to be so hard to take responsibility.

Accepting your role in your own failures doesn't mean beating yourself up about it. You simply have to identify where you are holding yourself back, acknowledge it and then take action to change it. It's not about the mistakes you've made or the actions you didn't take in the past. It's about what you do now to reach your goals.

Difficult Situations and Failures Build Character
Have you ever heard someone refer to a difficult situation or adversity as 'character building?' But what is character, really? And why would you want to build it?

Character is the person you are – and who others perceive you to be through your actions and your beliefs. When people say that something builds character, it's simply recognizing that dealing with and overcoming adversity builds the kind of mental toughness that you need for a self-disciplined life. Some of the most successful people have failed many times over before they found success. They just had the self-discipline to learn from their failures and to keep trying.

Self-discipline forms the basis of what we often think of as 'good character.' Self-disciplined people follow through on the promises they make; they don't drop projects when their enthusiasm wanes or let people down on plans. They get the task at hand done, and they are reliable. People with character have an inner strength and a resolve that comes from good discipline. Self-disciplined people naturally command respect from others and are better able to control their reactions to situations and events. They appear cool, calm and in control at all times.

To build that kind of character, most people have learned to endure difficult and uncomfortable situations. Luckily, they don't have to be the kind of life-threatening situations that you might encounter in the military!

Every time you push through discomfort and do something you didn't want to do or felt uncomfortable doing, your brain learns that it can be achieved. If you keep repeating that task, it will eventually become habitual behavior. So while you may never come to enjoy that task, you won't feel any kind of fear or resistance to completing it.

One thing that many people have a fear of is public speaking. While it's no military combat situation, it can bring out even the most confident of us in a cold sweat. It's normal to be nervous when you learn that you may need to stand in front of a room full of people and speak on a topic. Even if you're an expert on the topic!

However, as anyone who's done public speaking will tell you; while it is certainly nerve-wracking, once you've done it the sense of accomplishment is amazing, and it's really not all that bad once you begin to speak. The next time you're asked you'll be less reluctant. Plus, if you speak in public several times over a few months, you'll find that by the final event you'll have nothing more than the mildest pre-speaking nerves.

Get Comfortable Being Uncomfortable
Take a moment to consider: how comfortable are you with feeling uncomfortable?

It may seem like a ridiculous question. Surely if you feel uncomfortable, you are by definition not comfortable with it? But self-disciplined people have learned to live by the phrase *'feel the fear, and do it anyway.'* It's not that they don't feel uncomfortable, it's that they know that the personal growth they desire can only be found on the other side of the discomfort. And so, they get comfortable with feeling uncomfortable because they know it's temporary discomfort, and the outcome is worth it.

Think about it: if you'd never experienced any kind of uncomfortable situation, would you be prepared for adult life? If you'd never hurt yourself in any way, would you have the same appreciation for avoiding the physical danger that is essential to keep you alive?

Self-discipline is, by nature, uncomfortable. If it was easy, you wouldn't need self-discipline at all! In this book, we've looked at ways to harness and boost willpower, build habits, and look after yourself in order to either maximize or reduce the need for self-discipline. Yet, there are going to be situations that come up that will require you to handle unplanned discomfort. For these, you'll need straight-up self-discipline. Training yourself to get comfortable in tough situations will make it much easier to handle the inevitable setbacks and discomfort that life can throw at us. You need to build some endurance upfront by choosing to do things you don't necessarily want to.

Being disciplined means recognizing the initial discomfort as a sign that you're on the right track. That craving for a sugary doughnut? It's just telling you that you're on the right track with your healthy eating habits. Muscle soreness the day after a gym session? It's proof that your body is changing and becoming stronger. When you handle these everyday discomforts with discipline, they eventually fade and become almost unnoticeable. And you're building up the mental toughness you need to handle the more challenging, unpredictable situations that life might throw your way. It's character building, and eventually persevering will become your default mode.

Appreciating life's challenges for the opportunities they are, and applying self-discipline to complete them will allow you to grow as a person in the best possible way.

Getting comfortable with feeling uncomfortable is one of the best gifts you could ever give yourself.

Make a habit of not running from the uncomfortable opportunities that present themselves. Embrace them for the challenges they are, and each time you'll develop a little more mental toughness and all the benefits that come with pushing yourself outside of your comfort zone.

Build Your Endurance by Depriving Yourself
One way to train yourself to handle tough situations is to put yourself in a situation where you have to do without something that keeps you in your comfort zone.

For smartphone addicts, it could be a 48hr phone ban, where you switch off your device and leave it off for a full two days. It could be sugar, coffee, TV, or even choosing to walk everywhere instead of driving. Anything that makes your life more difficult than it normally is, and will force you to use your willpower. Of course, don't make the situation life-threatening, or dangerous to your health. You want to be uncomfortable, not full-out suffering.

Ideally, choose something that will give you more time or somehow contribute towards your life goals. If you want to lose weight, cutting out sugar might be a good choice. If you want to start your own business or write a book, ditching TV for a week might free up enough time to make some headway.

Cold Showers to Boost Self-discipline
It may sound slightly extreme, but another way to help you build mental toughness is to take a cold shower daily. You don't have to have a completely cold shower; turning the temperature down to the lowest setting for the last minute or two of your shower is a great way to get the benefits.

You're basically choosing to endure a difficult situation, and as we've just discussed, this is the best way to build endurance for other difficult tasks. Plus, not only do cold showers help you build self-discipline, but they also have some other interesting benefits, backed by science. Cold showers after exercising can decrease muscle soreness. Turning the temperature down can also help ease depression, improve circulation, keep your skin clear, and help you shed some excess weight.

An interesting study in the Netherlands in 2016 demonstrated evidence that cold showers improve your mental toughness. The participants were all split into four groups. The first three groups were assigned a length of time to take a cold shower, varying between 30 seconds and 90 seconds. The fourth group was a control group who showered as normal.

They completed this for 30 consecutive days, and then for another 30 days they showered however they liked. Over the course of the full 60 days, each participant was asked to fill in web-based surveys. The surveys revealed that the participants who took cold showers had 29% fewer sick days than the control group. What made this all the more interesting is that those people didn't report feeling any less sick than the people who took warm showers. They simply battled through feeling sick and still went to work.

Arguments about passing on germs to your co-workers aside, this study provides scientific evidence that proactively enduring difficult situations makes you more mentally tough in other situations.

So, if you want to start developing your mental toughness and your self-discipline, taking cold showers might be one of the easiest (if slightly uncomfortable) ways to do it.

Don't Forget Self-Care
It's important to remember to practice proper self-care. Placing yourself into uncomfortable situations is a great way to build mental toughness, but those situations should never be dangerous or unbearable.

If you're giving up TV, that's obviously not going to cause you any harm, but make sure you don't replace it with an unhealthy habit. Similarly, you might start a punishing exercise regime, but always seek the advice of your doctor and fitness professionals before you start on any kind of extreme exercise routine. Too much of a good thing can be bad for you. And, let's not forget that willpower is like a muscle. Yes, it can be made stronger, but it also fatigues. If you put too much pressure on your willpower all at once, it might prevent you from exercising willpower in other important situations.

Be uncomfortable, but listen to what your body and mind are telling you and be aware of the signals it's sending. There's a distinction between self-discipline and addiction or workaholism so pay attention and make sure that your mental toughness training is making you stronger, not weaker.

Real Life Case Study - John

John joined the military straight from high school and served for fifteen years. He was a good student in high school, and usually had the self-discipline to study. However, like most people, John wasn't 100% focused all of the time and rarely pushed himself outside of his comfort zone. During his time in the military, John learned many things about self-discipline and his personal capacity to handle situations. Over his fifteen years in service, he was thrust into various situations where his self-discipline was one of many life-saving skills he had to rely on. He learned a healthy respect for following rules, and how to handle uncomfortable situations.

When John eventually left the military after a life-changing injury, he took a job in an advertising office as a junior copywriter. He was starting from the bottom of the ladder and had a lot to learn. Many people would have found it incredibly daunting, especially as it was such a different role than serving in the military.

However, John had spent his whole working life handling discomfort of a much more extreme nature. Although he found it challenging, his time in the military had taught him how to push through uncomfortable situations. He spent long hours working on his writing, making sure each piece he wrote was just right for his clients.

His hard-earned self-discipline served him well, and he devoted most of his time to learning the craft of copywriting and completing a diploma via distance learning on top of his full-time job. Soon enough, his perseverance paid off, and he was writing campaigns that were making the agency's clients millions of dollars in profits. He found that his colleagues who considered him junior just a few months previously were coming to him for advice on their writing. After just three years at the agency, John as was promoted to the head of his department ahead of other, longer-serving colleagues. His success was only possible in such a short time frame because of his ability to be so self-disciplined – a skill he learned mostly in the military.

There's a lot to learn from the military about self-discipline. Luckily, you don't need to go through boot camp to take some of the lessons away and implement them into your own life.

In the next chapter, we'll take a look at one of the biggest enemies of productivity and self-discipline: ***procrastination.***

Chapter 7 : Defeating The Enemy; Procrastination

"Procrastination is the thief of time, collar him."
Charles Dickens, David Copperfield

Procrastination is the enemy of self-discipline, and of success. If you're a chronic procrastinator, you might believe that you're simply a lazy person. In fact, chronic procrastination might be the very habit that caused you to seek out advice on building self-discipline. You may be relieved to learn that procrastination isn't a sign of laziness and is instead a combination of many complex drivers that cause us to delay taking action. The good news is, once you understand what's keeping you stuck in procrastination mode, you'll be able to shake it off more easily.

You Think You're Lazy, But You're Actually Scared
This may sound ridiculous. There's probably no good reason for you to fear to get on with your tasks. Especially when those tasks are taking you closer to achieving the exciting goals you've set for yourself. So why then, do you find yourself continually pushing tasks aside to do other things that are less important?

The answer is fear. The primal kind of subconscious fear that your reptilian brain is designed to create, that you may not even be fully aware of as fear. It manifests itself as a resistance to complete a task or reach a goal that your reptilian brain recognizes as a threat. Unfortunately, the kind of thing it perceives as a threat can often be exactly what our conscious selves are aiming for!

Fear of Failure
One of the most common reasons for fear-related

procrastination is a fear of failure. It's also one of the easier types of procrastination-inducing fear to recognize. It's actually very common to procrastinate when you are not confident that you can succeed. You may be worried about not completing the task to the right standard. You may even be afraid that failing at this task may cause people to have a negative opinion of you.

For example, you may simply not run the marathon because you're worried you can't complete it in the time you want. You find excuses not to train and eventually, may even find a reason to not do it at all; because that seems preferable to being labeled as a failure.

Giving in to this kind of fear-driven procrastination means that you will never be able to complete anything of any great importance. Or it may cause you to delay taking action until the very last minute, meaning that ironically, you're more likely to fail.

If you find yourself in this situation, try sitting down and making a list of all the reasons you *are* likely to succeed. You should also make sure that your plan to achieve your goal is broken down into manageable steps. This will allow you to assess your progress regularly and adjust if you need to, in order to meet the end goal.

Accepting Failure
The main objective is, of course, to complete the task and succeed. However, it may also help to change your mindset around failure. Many of the most successful people in history experienced failure before achieving great success. In fact, their failures often became their stepping stones to success.

Instead of viewing all failure as a hindrance, try embracing it as a necessary step to success. If you can reframe failure as a vital part of the process of succeeding it will help you overcome fearing it.

Remember that not doing something is the biggest failure there is. If you do it and it's not perfect, then at the very worst you'll have learned something. In most cases, you'll simply be closer to eventual success. Very few people experience life without any failures, and it could be said that our lives are eventually all the richer for the failures that we do overcome.

Fear of Success
This fear can be harder to spot. It doesn't seem to make sense that success could be something that causes fear. It can take a lot of self-awareness to identify and combat this form of fear-driven procrastination. However, it is actually quite a common reason for procrastination. What makes us afraid of success can vary. It may be that if you get the promotion you want, you fear not being competent in your new role. Or you may worry about how your colleagues will view you if you become 'above' them.

Often the fear of success is tied to how others might react to that success. Most of us are comfortable with the relationships we have and want to keep them. If achieving your goals makes others view you differently., and changes your relationship with them, it can be a scary thought.

For your reptilian brain, remaining part of your *'tribe'* is crucial to your survival. Many millennia ago, a human without a tribe to rely on would be lucky to survive in the wilderness. Despite the fact that humans no longer live in the same way, your prehistoric reptilian brain doesn't recognize the difference. Anything that might threaten your relationship with your *'tribe'* is a serious threat to your reptilian brain– even if it's exactly what your conscious mind wants.

If your goals might make you more successful than your partner, friends, or family, your reptilian brain may try to shield you from the emotional pain of this. This is alongside trying to prevent you from being *'shunned'* from your tribe. This tends to manifest as procrastination, or some form of self-sabotage so that we don't have to deal with the consequences of success.

You may also be concerned about how becoming successful will change you. If your goals are related to making more money, you may have some limiting beliefs about money being evil, or rich people being greedy. These limiting beliefs can make you reluctant to actually make a lot of money, and are rarely easy to spot.

For this kind of fear, regular meditation can help you think more clearly and identify the root cause of your procrastination. The key is to sit quietly and think about your goals. Notice if there is any tension in your body when you think of what you want to achieve. Try to release that tension, and consider what is causing it. Journaling during this mediation can also help. By jotting down whatever is in your mind without trying to analyze or censor it, you may discover some surprising reasons why you are afraid of success.

Once you know what it is that you are scared of, it will be easier to overcome. If you've explored your reasons – your *'why'*- for each goal, reminding yourself of these should help also boost your motivation to achieve them.

Even understanding the root cause doesn't always make the fear go away, but it will help you see that it's often an unjustified fear. If you're feeling any kind of procrastination-causing fear, the best way to combat that is to just take a deep breath and get to work.

Other Reasons for Procrastination
Fear is the most common cause, but there are other drivers for procrastination. One of them is a lack of clarity. If the expected outcome for the task isn't clear, or it's a task that's unfamiliar to you, you may feel overwhelmed and put off beginning the task.

This type of procrastination is actually a close relative of the fear of failure. You're afraid that you don't know how to complete the task. So instead of seeking clarity, or just starting the task, you delay it until it can't possibly be delayed anymore.

Another issue that might cause procrastination is a lack of energy. If you feel too tired to do the task, you may put it off indefinitely. This is the closest procrastination driver to real laziness, but it often tends to be a sign that you aren't looking after yourself properly rather than a personality trait.

A healthy diet, exercise and a decent amount of sleep are crucial to having enough willpower to tackle tasks. Too much alcohol can leave you feeling foggy and lethargic the next day, even if you don't have a particularly bad hangover. Addressing any lifestyle issues should solve the problem of feeling too tired to complete tasks.

In some cases, an underlying health issue can cause fatigue. These include but are not limited to thyroid issues, depression and anemia. If you're experiencing persistent tiredness that isn't helped by improving your lifestyle, then seek advice from a medical professional.

Finally, your procrastination may be due to a lack of personal investment in the outcome. If you've explored your 'why' and set SMART goals, as we've covered in previous chapters, then you should have a good understanding of the benefits of reaching your goals.

If the tasks you are procrastinating on aren't linked in any way to your goals, try to find a positive link to the outcome. This should give you the motivation boost you need to complete them. Even the most mundane chores have a positive outcome if you look hard enough. For example, doing the laundry will mean that you will have a larger selection of clean clothing to look and feel your best. Going for that run will boost your energy, endorphins, and health and help you live a longer, healthier life.

Taking Back Control

Understanding why you are procrastinating is only part of the battle. Once you know what's holding you back, you need to take decisive action to stop procrastination in its tracks and get stuff done. Ultimately, overcoming procrastination is a question of self-discipline. When you find yourself procrastinating, you need to accept that is what you're doing. Then, make a decision to get on with the task you should be doing – and just do it.

Understanding why you are procrastinating can help you immensely, but don't let that in itself become a new procrastination tool! Even knowing why you're procrastinating won't help you if you don't apply the self-discipline to get the task done and overcome it.

But if you're reading this book, chances are you don't yet have the willpower of steel. So here are some more general techniques that can help you beat procrastination.

Do The Worst Tasks First

It's often just human nature to put off doing the tasks we least enjoy. It could be a manager leaving it to the last minute to deliver the news that there won't be an annual pay rise. Or a housewife who hates emptying the dishwasher and leaves it to the last minute. We all have some tasks that we always tend to put off because we don't enjoy them.

The problem with doing it this way is that the task looms over us, sucking some of the joy out of the 'nice' tasks that we prioritize. This feeling of dread or guilt for leaving the task until last can be even worse when the task is important or urgent. Such as the case of the manager putting off delivering the bad news of no pay rise.

It's a *terrible* strategy.

The best way to tackle it is to identify your worst tasks and get them done and out of the way as soon as you can. The added bonus to this is that the sense of pride and relief at getting them out of the way will give you a surge of motivation. That boost should help you to get through the rest of your tasks.

Tackling the toughest tasks first will make the rest of your day feel easy. Even better, over time it becomes a habit – which as we've already learned makes self-discipline so much easier!

The 2-Minute Rule

Similar to doing the worst task first, the 2-minute rule states that if a task will take you 2 minutes or less, you should do it immediately. It makes sense, but often we tend to push these to the bottom of the list *because* they are such quick tasks – which means they can get forgotten.

Getting a few quick tasks ticked off your to-do list will make you feel like you are accomplishing more. In turn, this will boost your motivation to tackle the bigger things on the list.

So, pay that bill, call that company, clean the vacuum filter. Whatever you have noted down to do later that's a 2-minute task, get it done immediately. You'll get a nice motivation boost, *and* you won't risk the stress of it not being done at all because you kept pushing it down the list.

Break Tasks Down Into Smaller Pieces

Sometimes a task seems so large that it's overwhelming. So, we put it off to the last minute or don't do it at all because we're avoiding dealing with our fear of the task. The best way to reduce the fear is to break the job into manageable steps.

This works best with really big tasks and goals, but it can also be applied to smaller jobs if you're really resisting starting them. Once the task is a series of small steps, it will be much less daunting. There's also the added benefit that with each step you complete, you will get a little motivation boost that spurs you on to complete the other steps.

You can also commit to doing just one step if you still feel resistance to the task. Once you've completed just one step, the chances are that you will feel able to do the next one, and the next one. Before you know it the job will be completed.

If you don't know how to break the job down into manageable steps, then just identify the first and smallest action you can take to move the task along. Then the next smallest action, and so on. For example, if you're planning a party, you might break it down into food, decorations, invitations, etc.

By tackling just one small step at a time, before you know it the whole job will have been completed.

Don't Be Too Hard On Yourself
You might think that chastising yourself for procrastinating and being hard on yourself is the best way to instill the self-discipline to get things done. But numerous studies have shown that berating yourself for procrastinating actually makes you more likely to continue procrastinating.

One study from the University of Carleton showed that self-forgiveness was actually key to avoiding future procrastination among students. While it was common for the students to procrastinate about studying for the first exam, those who were hard on themselves were more likely to not study for subsequent exams. Those who procrastinated on the first exam but forgave themselves and didn't feel guilty about it were much less likely to procrastinate on the next exam.

The same holds true for studies on dieting. People who feel guilty for breaking the 'rules' of their diet are much more likely to keep eating badly or drop the diet altogether than those who forgave themselves.

Make Your Goals Known
Another method for keeping yourself on track is to let

others know your goals. When your family and friends are aware of what you are aiming to achieve, it will make you feel more accountable for achieving it.

Avoiding a loss of face can sometimes be a powerful motivator for the right personality types. There's also the added benefit that some of your friends and family members may be able to offer support and assistance to reach your goals. If someone you know has a similar goal, you could even consider getting a specific accountability partner so that you can both keep each other on track. By setting up regular milestones, or indulging in some friendly competition you might be able to bolster your willpower that little bit more.

Real Life Case Study – Julia

Julia was a history student in her final year of college, and she was finding it difficult to stop procrastinating on studying for her final exams. Despite desperately wanting to pass with good grades, she would find herself socializing or surfing the internet instead of studying.

Even though she was feeling terribly guilty about the time she was wasting, Julia continued to procrastinate and found her anxiety levels were rising. To *'make more time for study'* she would stay up late, but instead of studying, she would watch movies all night.

Over time the late nights compounded by the guilt and anxiety left Julia exhausted and worried that she would fail the exams. At her wit's end, she sought advice from the college counselor on how to get over her procrastination problem.

The counselor helped her identify that her procrastination was due to a combination of issues. Julia was afraid of failing the exams and disappointing her parents, as she would be the first child of her family to complete a college degree. She was also afraid of success because getting good grades would put her in a better position career-wise than her siblings. She feared that this might affect her relationship with them.

These fear issues were made worse by Julia's habit of staying up late and not getting enough sleep, which left her too tired to tackle studying the next day. As she had been putting off the studying, over time, it had become an almost insurmountable task in Julia's mind. She was worried that she may never be able to catch up in time.

The counselor helped Julia work through her fear issues and concentrate on the positive outcomes of passing the exams. She helped Julia forgive herself for her earlier procrastination and to focus on positive steps for the future. She also helped her work out a study plan that broke the studying down into small and manageable steps by dividing it into topics.

The study plan listed the topics Julia found most challenging to be completed first, to get those out of the way and reduce the overwhelm. It also allowed adequate time for sleep, socializing and moderate exercise so that fatigue wasn't preventing her from focusing. Julia had regular meetings with the counselor to discuss her progress against the study plan, which kept her accountable and helped her to stay on track.

By applying all of the counselor's advice and applying some self-discipline to knuckle down to studying, Julia was able to get over her procrastination habit. She eventually passed her final exams with excellent grades.

Ultimately, while you can use some of the tips in this chapter to beat procrastination, it's up to you to apply willpower and self-discipline to stop putting things off.

In the next chapter, we'll look at the 3 key steps to self-discipline. These incorporate some of the tools and techniques we've already explored along with some new ones to help you build your self-disciplined life.

Chapter 8 : Three Key Steps to Self-Discipline

"Discipline is the bridge between goals and accomplishment."
Jim Rohn

So far, we've covered the science behind self-discipline and looked at some practical ways to set yourself up for success in your newly self-disciplined life.

In this chapter, we'll be summarizing some of the key points, and covering new points as we look at the 3 key steps to self-discipline. If you're still not even close to implementing a more self-disciplined approach to life, consider this chapter as the blueprint to get you started.

Step One: Decide What You Want
In many respects, this comes under what we learned in Chapter 4 about choosing goals and understanding your 'why.' But one additional key part to this step is that you must DECIDE.

Wanting something is very different to firmly *deciding* you will achieve it. A decision is a commitment to making the necessary changes and doing the necessary work - no matter what. Without a committed decision then your efforts are almost certainly doomed to fail. A want without a decision is simply a wish, and the old adage 'if wishes were horses, beggars would ride' holds some truth. Most of us can name something we *want* to achieve with all our hearts – but few of us truly decide to achieve it.

Simply setting goals and reading self-development books won't help until you make a firm decision to commit to change. Once you've fully committed to your decision to live a more self-disciplined life, implementing it will become much easier. Until you commit, it's still only something you want to do.

Of course, in order to make a truly committed decision, it needs to be a decision you can fully get behind. Without investigating your real reasons why you want to achieve the goal, a fully committed decision won't be possible. So, while the decision and the 'why' are two separate steps, they are very closely linked.

Make today the day that you make the firm decision that you're not just going to try to achieve your goals. You **are** going to achieve your goals. Commit to the fact that you are not going to let anybody or anything stand in your way.

Once you've decided to commit to your goal, there are several ways that you can strengthen your resolve:

Get Emotionally Engaged With Your Goal
When you set your goals and visualized how it would feel to achieve it, you began the process of becoming emotionally engaged with your goal. In order to maintain a commitment to your goal, you should be regularly revisiting that exercise of visualizing what success looks and feels like. However, this is just one step to becoming emotionally engaged with your goal.

It's important to not only be engaged with the successful outcome of the goal but to also engage fully with the process of getting there. If you're not passionate or excited about the journey to achieve the goal, you'll be relying on willpower alone to get you to the end result. And as we've already learned, willpower is a finite resource.

We've already covered tips and tricks to increase or

conserve your willpower, but circumventing willpower altogether is always the best course of action. When you can find the joy in the journey, willpower is no longer necessary. If you can learn to love the process as much as the expected outcome, then you are already halfway to success. Learn to love exercise, healthy cooking, early morning runs, and any other necessary tasks that move you towards your end goal.

Of course, sometimes some hardcore old-school self-discipline is needed. If there is no physical activity you enjoy, but your health is suffering, you have to exercise or suffer the health consequences. However, do your best to find joy in every process. It makes all the difference to how self-disciplined you can be.

Re-Commit To Your Goals Daily
Write down your goals daily in your journal to make sure that they are always firmly in the forefront of your mind. Spending time at the end of each day to reflect on your goals can also help to keep you accountable and prevent you from making bad decisions. It can help provide the motivation you need to take consistent action and remind yourself what you are aiming for and why. Keeping your goals at the forefront of your mind is always a good idea. The more your goals are ingrained into your consciousness, the greater chance you have of staying consistent and achieving it.

Make a decision to do everything possible not to allow excuses to become acceptable.

Make Success Your Obsession
Obsession can often be looked at as a negative thing, but most obsession is a perfectly healthy situation. In fact, many successful business leaders – for example, Grant

Cardone in his book, *"Be Obsessed or Be Average"* - credit their obsession as the key to their success.

The negative side of obsession is the clinical kind of obsession we think of in relation to disorders like OCD and anorexia. That kind of obsession is uncontrollable. Non-clinical obsession is simply a passion for something, and it's this kind of obsession that propels people to success. The dictionary definition of obsession is simply, *"the domination of one's thoughts or feelings by a persistent idea, image, or desire."*

Consider any great athlete. They are likely to be naturally gifted at their chosen sport, but without an obsessive attitude towards practicing, they would have been unlikely to make it to a professional level.

So, take a leaf out of Grant Cardone's book and become (healthily) obsessed with your goals. When you find yourself with spare time or resources, use them toward taking you a step further to your goal.

What If You Just Can't Find Your Passion For The Process?
You may find it difficult to find the joy in the process of achieving your goals. You might even find yourself constantly coming up with excuses as to why you can't take consistent action towards them. In this situation, you need to consider if these are truly goals you wish to achieve.

Prioritize Properly
Getting your priorities straight is very important when you need to be more self-disciplined. You only have a finite amount of time and willpower, and you need to make the most of those limited resources. Your priority tasks should always be the tasks that move you towards your goals.

Trying to do *everything* just doesn't work, so if you lead a busy life, the first thing to tackle is your prioritization.

Take the time to complete a prioritization exercise where you write down all of the tasks you complete for a week, and how long you spend on them. Include all tasks: work, chores, social time, organizing household matters, rest, relaxation and even any obvious procrastination activities. Be honest when you complete this as you don't have to share it with anyone. There's no point in lying to yourself. In order to get the best out of this exercise, you need to have an accurate picture of how much time you spend on the various activities that make up your days.

Keep it simple. It doesn't need to be a very detailed account and whichever way you choose to log it should be as easy to fit into your day as possible. It could be jotting it down in a notepad that you keep with you, or it could be logged in the notes section on your smartphone. If you are a whizz with spreadsheets, you may want to create a spreadsheet for yourself. It doesn't matter *how* you record it as long as it's recorded in a way that is clear and easy for you to read back later.

Once you've logged all of your activities for the week, take a look and analyze where your time is being spent. Take note of whether the most time is being spent on tasks that are a priority. Of course, there are always some tasks that are not specifically priorities, but that cannot be removed or avoided. These are tasks which are not moving you closer towards some higher goal- but that are essential to daily living. Tasks such as chores, attending your regular job, and self-care fall under this umbrella. Where you can see the opportunity to complete those tasks more efficiently or to delegate activities like chores, then you should aim to do so.

Identify where you are spending time on activities that don't need to be completed and also don't move you towards any higher goals. This could be time spent on social media, watching television, playing games, and any time that you feel is potentially 'wasted.'

These are tasks that should be eliminated if possible and should certainly be reduced to make way for priority tasks. Be careful not to remove all self-care and relaxation activities – as we discussed in Chapter 3, it's essential to look after yourself.

Is It Ever Appropriate To Quit?
So, you've identified your goals. You know your *'why.'* You've found the joy in the process. And you've prioritized effectively. In most instances, these are the foundations you need to propel you towards success. But sometimes your circumstances, and therefore your priorities can change.

For example, goals that provide joy and inspiration during a time in your life when you are single and child-free may well change once you meet a partner and/or have children. These kinds of life events don't *always* change your goals, but they can have a profound impact on your personal values and lifestyle; and in turn, on the life you wish to create for yourself.

In these circumstances, there is absolutely no shame or failure in reassessing your priorities and changing your goals - regardless of whether you achieved the original goal. The whole point of being more self-disciplined is to create for yourself the life that you want to live. If your perception of what an ideal life looks like changes, then it is only natural and right that your goals change to accommodate that.

While it's fine to adjust your goals and even to scrap some of them entirely under the right circumstances, try not to ditch goals for the wrong reasons. For example:

- they seem too hard to reach
- you're distracted by a new idea or theory
- your family and friends aren't supporting you in your goal

A large part of self-discipline is not allowing yourself to make excuses for not reaching your goals. If you've made a firm decision to achieve them, then unless you've experienced a major life change, there should be no reason at all to quit.

Step Two: Prepare And Plan For Taking Action
So, you've decided you are going to achieve your goal, and you're committed to a successful outcome.
Congratulations, you're well on the way to success!
However, it's now time to deal with the practicalities of preparing and planning the actions and resources you need to be successful. Most people fall into two distinct camps. Some of us love to prepare and plan. In fact, some of us get so preoccupied with preparing and planning that we never truly move on from this stage! And others tend to rush into situations with barely a thought of how to get there or what practical resources they will need to achieve success.

Effective preparation and planning are crucial to providing the right framework for eventual success.

Effective Planning
You should have an overall plan setting out timescales and actionable steps between when you intend to begin and

when you attend to achieve your goal. You should also aim to break it down into monthly, weekly and potentially even daily targets or commitments, depending on the goal.

Your plan should be realistic, and able to fit in with your schedule. Planning to exercise for two hours a day when that's the only free time you have is setting your plan up to fail. It would be much better to allocate a consistent 30 minutes as you would be less likely to find a reason not to do it. There are numerous studies showing that just the act of planning the work can make you much more likely to complete it. A study of young people and exercise discovered that young people were more likely to exercise when they wrote down a detailed plan beforehand. The young people were split into three groups, one of which (Group A) was asked at the beginning of each week to write down exactly when and where they intended to exercise.

The other two groups either tracked their exercise (Group B) or tracked their exercise and also received motivational materials (Group C). Group A – the group that wrote down when and where they would exercise were much more successful at actually exercising than either of the other two groups.

Breaking Tasks Down
In order to make your goal manageable and to be able to plan effectively, you'll normally need to break it down into smaller steps. This serves many purposes; including making the goals seem more achievable, allowing you to schedule the right amount of time for each step and also to identify any dependencies.

Sometimes a particular action or mini-goal needs to be achieved before you can move on to the next step. Planning these out in advance means that you remove the risk of accidentally skipping a step and having to re-plan.

For example, a goal to run your own fashion drop-shipping company might be broken down into several steps or stages like this:

- Identify profitable product niches
- Create a brand logo and identity
- Create a six-month marketing plan
- Set up social media campaigns
- Build and test the website
- Launch website

The exact steps will depend on your goal and your existing level of skill or knowledge in that field that you can call upon. It's also likely that each step will need its own detailed plan. For example:

Identify profitable product niches could be planned out in greater detail like this:

- **Week 1** – Research trending hashtags on Instagram to find on-trend products. Identify at least six potential products to launch with.
- **Week 2** – Investigate profit margins on the potential products, and list them in order of profit margins.
- **Week 3** – research potential competitors and their price ranges

Some goals don't automatically lend themselves to be broken down into steps. For example, if your goal is to run for fifteen minutes every single day, chances are that you don't need to build that up in increments, do any research, or develop any special skills beforehand. However, you *can* plan out the times you will run and if they differ each day, and also ensure that you have appropriate clothing to go running in the various weather conditions you may encounter over a year.

Spending some time thinking about the detail of how you will achieve the goal, and making sure you have access to any equipment or resources you need is always time well spent.

Step Three: ACT!
The third and final step is to take action to implement your plan. It's amazing how many people lay out clear and thorough plans, but never actually take any of the action laid out in those plans. I've stressed the importance of deciding and planning so far in this chapter, but all of the deciding and preparing won't amount to anything without action. This is the most crucial of all the three steps. Action is the only step that can never be missed out if you want to succeed.

You can act without a plan. You can even take action without making a firm decision to see the goal through to the end. But without action, you can never succeed regardless of how lucky you are.

So How Do You Make Sure That You Stick To Your Plan And Act?
If you've completed the deciding and planning stages, a lot of the mental burden of taking action is removed. You know you are going to do it, you know how and when you're going to do it. Technically, there should be no real barriers to just getting on and doing it.

Try not to leave too long between the planning step and

acting, as you'll lose some of your momentum before you get the chance to convert the task into a habit. Losing momentum early on will make it much harder to start up again at a later date. The best way to stick to your plan is to simply begin implementing it immediately. The first few weeks are always the hardest, and putting off starting will only make it harder. Take advantage of the motivation you have now and jump straight in!

What To Do When Things Don't Go To Plan

So you've put in the painstaking work of proper planning and preparation. Yet somehow, circumstances outside of your control or that you could not have foreseen are impacting your well-laid plans.

Don't panic!

The fact is, life happens. While you should avoid making excuses for not taking action, if there is a genuine and legitimate reason that your plans are not going as expected then don't be too hard on yourself.

This is where resilience, flexibility, and adaptability come into play. We all encounter circumstances like this occasionally and having the adaptability to deal with them is essential. The key thing is to not give up. If necessary, you can return to the planning and preparation stage and rethink the entire plan. In most cases, a few simple tweaks to your plan can have you back on course for success in no time. Depending on the situation it may be that you simply need to pause your plan for a brief amount of time. Alternatively, you may simply need to add additional steps, change a couple of existing steps, or come up with a way to make the plan work under a new set of circumstances.

Remember that being hard on yourself doesn't improve

your self-discipline. When things don't go to plan, forgive yourself and focus on doing what you need to in order to get back on track.

Real Life Case Study – Julia

Julia had a plan, and she was committed to seeing it through. Her goal was to reach a target weight of 150 pounds within 12 months – in time for her 40th birthday. After consulting a dietician and doing extensive research on health and fitness, Julia identified that her target was perfectly achievable. Julia set a plan that involved losing 2 pounds per week on average.

With the help of a dietician, Julia devised a diet that kept her calorie intake low enough to encourage 2 pounds of weight loss, but high enough to ensure that she wasn't risking any nutritional deficiencies or otherwise damaging her health. Julia's plan also included incorporating exercise sessions five times per week. Initially, she committed fully to her goal and was able to stay on track, losing 1.5-2.5 pounds per week.

Unfortunately, shortly after the first three months, Julia had an accident at work and broke her right wrist. As a right-handed person, not only did this impact on Julia's training schedule, it also affected her ability to prepare healthy food.

It would have been easy for Julia to wallow in self-pity, live on take-out and skip the exercise until her wrist had healed. However, because Julia had made a committed decision to achieve her goal, she was not prepared to allow this setback to prevent her from reaching it.

Julia met with a personal trainer who specialized in working with people who had injuries. He helped devise an exercise routine that allowed her to exercise without causing pain or risking further damage in her broken wrist. The personal trainer recommended a mix of lower body exercises and low impact cardio that Julia could do without risk of further injury to her wrist.

Julie also met with a dietician to find ways that she could meet her nutritional needs by sourcing healthy but convenient foods that were pre-prepared where possible. Julia's budget constraints prevented her from having a full meal preparation service. However, with a little creativity and lots of research, she was able to come up with a suitable diet plan. Her new plan would still meet her nutritional needs and keep her calorie intake at the right level to maintain a weight loss.

Julia's wrist took three months to be healed to the point where she was able to resume cooking her own healthy meals and resume her old training regime. Because she had applied self-discipline and remained fully committed to her decision to reach her goal, Julia had managed to stay on track, continuing to lose an average of 2 pounds per month.

As a result of her resilience and flexibility, Julia was able to meet her overall weight goal within the 12 months. She was able to begin her 40's feeling healthy and full of confidence when it would have been so easy to allow the timescales to slip, or her weight to increase.

Now that you know the 3 key steps to self-discipline, it's time to move on to the final chapter. In Chapter 9 we'll be looking at how you can use momentum to ensure success.

Chapter 9 : Maintaining Momentum

"When you find yourself in the thickness of pursuing a goal or dream, stop only to rest. Momentum builds success."
Suzy Kassem

The Importance Of Momentum
In physics, momentum indicates how difficult an object is to stop. The more momentum an object has, the harder it will be to stop.

The same applies to your personal goals. The more momentum you have in your actions towards your goals, the more difficult it will be for outside forces to interfere with your determination to succeed.

The scientific equation to work out momentum is: **velocity x mass = momentum.**

In terms of personal momentum, you could consider the equation to be:
commitment x motivation = momentum.

New habits need a huge amount of willpower and energy just to begin. Then, once you've started, it's easy to allow it to trail off and make excuses - unless you know a few tricks to build and maintain the momentum.

Some people will start many projects and ventures in their lifetime, but never finish any of them. If this sounds like you, then it's possible that the problem is that you never built enough momentum to carry them through to the end.

Getting started is the hardest part, but once you do, momentum will start to build. This is the key to sticking with it until it becomes a fully formed habit. In this chapter, we'll look at the secrets of building and maintaining momentum.

Keeping The Momentum Going

You may need to make a big effort to begin taking action, but it's the small, consistent movements forward that make a lasting difference and keep the momentum going. And like a snowball rolling down a hill, if you can get off to a good enough start, the momentum you achieve can cause incredible growth and progress. Crucially, this is all without needing to rely too much on willpower.

Here are a few tips to make sure that once you have set the ball rolling, you keep on gathering momentum to propel you towards your goal:

Celebrate Your Progress

It's important to recognize the progress you are making, even if it's not huge steps. We often don't stop to celebrate the smaller successes as they don't feel like they're making a huge difference. Yet, it's these small steps that do eventually add up to big success.

Researchers from Harvard University Business School discovered that the key to productivity and happiness is to recognize your progress every day. To do this, keep a running list of your progress – like the opposite of a to-do list, this will be your 'done it' list. As the list grows, so will your confidence. And in turn, your motivation to keep making these small steps to success will increase.

You can enhance the momentum further by rewarding yourself for making progress – but make sure that the rewards themselves fit with your goals. For example, you wouldn't reward yourself for reaching a healthy blood pressure through diet and exercise by eating burgers loaded with fat and salt all week. Instead, you might reward yourself with a spa day or a trip somewhere nice.

Taking Small Steps Adds Up To Big Progress
If you're aiming for great things, it can be daunting to look at the overall goal; especially in the early stages. For example, if you're aiming to run a marathon in under 2 hours, and your current time is over 5 hours, the goal may seem incredibly far away.

If you focus on taking action, even if it feels like a small action, it will create some momentum. Almost all big goals are reached by taking incremental steps, and if you keep this in mind, the overall goal should feel less daunting.

Keep taking those little steps, and before you know it you'll have reached your big goal

Mindset Is Crucial
Keeping a positive mindset and preventing self-doubt or limiting beliefs from creeping in is very important to maintain momentum.

Pay attention to your internal dialogue and when you notice that you are beginning to allow your internal dialogue to become negative, make a conscious switch to a more positive tone. When your self-talk is self-defeating, it's almost impossible to keep up your momentum.

Watch out for resistance showing up that tries to justify why you shouldn't – or can't do something. For example, the voice of resistance in your mind might say *'it's too cold to go outside for a run,'* or *'surely it wouldn't hurt to just skip today's planned writing session?'*

It's up to you to stay strong and change that pattern. Change the dialogue in your mind to be positive instead: *'running in the cold will be so invigorating!'* or *'I feel like today's writing session will be really productive.'*

Daily affirmations can help keep your mindset positive and help you focus on staying on track for your goals. The best affirmations are specific, positive and usually start with 'I.' They should also be present tense. For example:

'I wake up full of energy and ready to begin my day with exercise.'
'I enjoy writing, and I'm lucky to be able to make time to write every single day.'
'I show up with intention at work and make a positive difference every day.'

You can find affirmations on the internet, but the best ones are personal to you, so why not write 3-4 of your own? Repeat them – aloud or in your head – several times each day.

Surround Yourself With Positive People
It's important to tackle your own mindset – after all, you spend all of your time in your own company. But it's also important to pay attention to the other people in your life, and how positive or supportive they are of your goals.

You can work on your own negative self-talk, but if your friends or family make negative comments, or don't support you in your goals, it will become difficult to keep up your momentum. Try and surround yourself with people who will act as your cheerleaders, and who are aiming for lofty goals themselves. It's often said that we become like the people we surround ourselves with, so whenever possible choose to spend your time with positive and self-disciplined people.

If there are others who share similar goals, consider becoming each other's accountability partner. Having somebody else on a similar journey to discuss and compare progress with can be very motivating. It also allows you to each tap into a little of the other's momentum to keep yourselves on track.

What To Do When Momentum Stops

With the best will in the world, sometimes life happens. If circumstances happen that are out of your control, it can sometimes derail your attempts at self-discipline, and wipe out all the momentum you've already built.

Some examples of circumstances that might stop your momentum:
- You, or a close friend or family member falling ill
- Meeting a new partner
- The end of a relationship
- Starting a family
- Being laid off at work
- Being promoted at work

It's important to note that not all of these are negative events, and not all of them are out of your control. Regardless, they can still all stop your momentum because they change your status quo, your focus, and potentially drastically change your lifestyle. Sometimes you'll have some time to plan and prepare beforehand, for example, if you're starting a family. However, that time isn't always enough. One way to mitigate the risk is to start with as much momentum as you possibly can.

The more momentum you create early on, the more it builds. Just like with a physical object that has gathered a large amount momentum it takes a very large outside force to stop you when you've built a lot of momentum.

How To Get It Back
Once you lose momentum, it can be very hard to get started again. As noted by Isaac Newton in his first law of motion also known as the law of inertia. A body at rest tends to remain at rest. Unless it is acted upon by an external force.

Commit To Starting Again
Your original momentum came from your initial action, spurred on by making a firm decision and planning.

If you've lost some momentum or worse, stopped altogether, then you'll need to try and regain the momentum. According to Isaac Newton, an object in motion will tend to stay in motion. So, if you can just take the first steps by committing to a small amount of action towards your goal, you can usually re-create enough momentum to keep things going.

The good news is that you've started before – so you know it's possible! Once you expend the energy to begin, that momentum will likely carry you through to complete even more.

Revisit Your Motivation
When you've lost momentum, your motivation can take a knock too. Reminding yourself of why you were trying to achieve your goal in the first place can help you find the willpower to pick up where you left off.

Revisit your journals where you recorded your daily progress, and see how far you've already come. Try to remember how it felt to be logging progress towards the goal, as well as visualizing how it will feel to actually reach your goal.

If you're a visual person, create a vision board that provides a visual representation of what your life will look like when you reach your goal. If your goals are related to money, it may be a nice house, car, or other items you wish to buy. If your goals are health related, then perhaps it's activities you'll be able to enjoy when you're fitter and stronger. Or clothes that you want to wear when you reach a goal body weight.

Don't forget that wanting to avoid negative consequences can also be a powerful short-term motivator that can give your momentum a kick-start. For example, not reaching your goal might have a negative consequence like not being able to afford something you need. In this case, you can tap into that to get yourself motivated enough to at least begin working towards your goal again.

Break It Into Smaller Goals
This tip has cropped up a few times – but it's particularly relevant when you're trying to build momentum back quickly.

In fact, according to laws of physics, the larger the object, the more difficulty it has building momentum. The same can be applied to goals. The larger the goal you are aiming for, the harder it will be to build up the momentum it's going to take to get you to your destination.

By breaking it into smaller goals, it's easier to get started and you have the added benefit that you can leverage the snowball effect.

Continuous Action and Improvement

Momentum is great for keeping you on track, and when you've built good habits, you'll barely have to think about knuckling down to your tasks. However, we all face days where even a fully formed habit isn't enough to keep us going purely on auto-pilot.

Persistence and avoiding excuses and justifications is key. If you've been tracking your progress and are ahead of schedule to meet your goal, don't use it as a justification to 'take a break' from your plan. Remember your decision to succeed and resist the urge to 'reward' yourself by slowing down your momentum. Stay consistent no matter what, self-discipline is all about being action oriented. Self-disciplined people decide to achieve their goal, and they don't stop taking action towards that goal until it's finished. Another problem with skipping days here and there is that if you do it too often, the skipping becomes a habit in itself!

Responsibilities can sometimes get in the way of taking consistent action. Most people have a lot of responsibilities, and it can be easy to let those responsibilities get in the way of your goals. Often, we do this because we consider our responsibilities towards other people to be more important than our responsibility to ourselves.

Don't be afraid to put yourself first. If you're self-disciplined, then you keep your promises to yourself. Don't let yourself down.

Raising The Bar

When you start to gather momentum, you'll probably find that you complete your tasks quicker than when you started. For example, if you set yourself a target of writing 300 words a day, you might find that in the beginning it took you an hour. However, after a while, it may only be taking you half an hour.

When this happens, you have two choices: stick to the plan, or raise the bar. The best choice is almost always to raise the bar. So, sticking with our writing example, you've already carved out an hour to write your 300 words – so why not commit to 600? That way, you'll reach your goal in half the time! It might be tempting to stick with the 300 words and add in working on a new or different goal for half an hour but this increases your chances of failing at both goals. Trying to implement too many new habits or working on too many goals at once is likely to lead to burnout or overwhelm.

Stick to the one goal but either reduce the timeframe or increase your end target to leverage the momentum you've already built.

Real Life Case Study – The Magic Of Momentum

David wanted to write a novel. He'd had his novel outlined for over a year, but it was still sat languishing in his desk drawer. Whenever David set goals, he always put finishing his novel on the list of things he wanted to achieve – and yet every time he never managed to get off the starting block.

On his 34th birthday, David decided that he needed to finish his novel. He wanted to be a traditionally published author before his 40th birthday and to do that he'd need at least one finished novel to send to agents and publishers. Once again, he wrote down his goal, but this time it was the only goal on the list.

The difference this time was that David wasn't just tapping into his wish to write a novel – he was making a fully focused and committed decision to finish the novel. He worked out that he had enough time to devote at least one hour a day purely to writing. With this in mind, he laid out a plan that would see him finish his 90,000-word first draft in six months.

He set himself a target of writing 500 words per day, every single day and created a progress chart for the wall of his office. He filled in the chart at the end of each writing session with his word count to date. Every 3,000 words he would reward himself with a lunchtime writing session and lunch in his favorite café.

He set himself affirmations that he repeated each morning, and he remained committed even when he sometimes didn't feel like writing. No matter what, every single day he found time to write 500 words before he went to bed.

In the beginning, he found it difficult to avoid the lure of temptations like unplanned social events or watching the latest TV series that his colleagues discussed at work. However, he'd taken steps to build and keep his momentum, and that ensured that he didn't give in.

After a couple of months, his consistent action had led to his writing becoming a habit. Seeing his progress chart fill up each day with word counts higher than his projections kept the momentum building. When he was consistently writing 800 words per writing session, he upped his target and continued to raise the bar whenever he hit a wordcount streak.

By the time four months had passed, David had already finished his first draft and was ready to edit and revise it. Because he'd built up so much momentum towards his goal, he was able to apply enough self-discipline to edit alongside writing 800 words a day towards his next novel.

By the time he reached his 35th Birthday, David had two finished manuscripts to send to agents and publishers and was already working on a third.

Conclusion: Your New Level of Self-Discipline Starts Here

Hopefully, you'll have already taken some action towards building a self-disciplined life while reading this book. However, if you've yet to take action now is the perfect time to begin.

In this book, we've covered everything you need in order to be the best you can be, including:

- The science of self-discipline and the different psychological theory models
- How your mindset affects your ability to achieve your goals
- The importance of proper self-care
- How to set effective goals
- The power of habits
- How to understand and avoid procrastination
- Why resolutions don't work
- How exercise can bring about immediate improvements in self-discipline
- The 3 key steps for self-discipline
- Building and maintaining momentum

But all of this knowledge won't help you if you don't take positive action and implement the tips and suggestions outlined in this book.

It's time to take control and step into your own greatness. You *can* be one of those people who appears to be 'naturally' self-disciplined. All you have to do is decide.

www.ingramcontent.com/pod-product-compliance
Lightning Source LLC
Chambersburg PA
CBHW030703220526
45463CB00005B/1887